Google Compliance Secrets

GOOGLE COMPLIANCE

SECRETS

The **Ultimate Marketing Playbook** to **Stay Google Compliant, Never Get Banned**, And **Access Hidden Google Ads Traffic** Reserved Only For Trustworthy Advertisers

DATHEN FAIRLEY

For more information, email dathen@compliancesecrets.com.

Hardcover ISBN: 978-1-954398-00-9

Paperback ISBN: 978-1-954398-01-6

eBook ISBN: 978-1-954398-02-3

IS YOUR WEBSITE GOOGLE COMPLIANT?
TAKE MY POLICY VIOLATION QUIZ TO FIND OUT
GOOGLE ADS POLICY VIOLATION QUIZ

Learn if your website is violating Google policies, which policy you are in danger of breaking, and what section in the book covers how to fix it. I've found readers who take the quiz before reading the book can implement the lessons learned in this book faster and are more successful getting back on Google Ads.

Take the quiz here:
www.compliancesecrets.com/quiz

Dedication

I dedicate this book to all the entrepreneurs who stuck their necks out to start a small business. The risk-takers who spend countless nights working, trying to figure out how to be successful doing something they didn't know how to do, but they did it anyway. For all of you who went into debt, who almost lost your marriage, and who had to apologize countless times to your children for working most of the day, every day, this is my way of saying "Thank You." Thank you for blazing a trail for all those who wish to follow in your footsteps. Thank you for showing us we desire a better life, a better retirement, and more control over this invisible depreciating asset called time.

A very special "Thank You" to Mark Hoverson, my very first mentor, who taught me how to use pay-per-click and Google AdWords. I credit Mark for blazing my trail and helping me get here today. He is no longer with us, but the fire he sparked in my heart still burns bright today for entrepreneurship and internet marketing. May your spirit continue to watch over my career from Heaven.

Google Compliance Secrets
Table of Contents

Preface

"Get 10,000 internet marketers back on Google Ads."

That is the goal I set for myself when I decided to write this book. If I was going to take the time to pour out over eleven years of experience, success, failure, blood, sweat, and tears about how to become Google compliant into a book, I wanted a massive impact across the marketing world. I tried to set a goal so high that if I succeed, I will have made my mark on the internet marketing world.

But even now, although I know I can do it, I can feel that little tingle of fear shooting up my spine. The self-talk in the back of my mind is trying to convince me not to move forward because of the magnitude of the goal. But this is how I know that what I am doing is good. I have learned that to be successful, you need a healthy dose of crazy thinking. You should create goals to help people that are so large, they scare you. It is human nature only to do things that have no risk of pain, anxiety, or failure, only things you think you can control. If we can't control something, we feel anxious and scared, which ultimately leads to selfish thinking, meaning we only look out for ourselves and resist looking to help other people. However, always being in control and being selfish will not lead you to success.

Over the years, I have created three digital marketing agencies, and even though I have had tremendous success, each of those businesses hit a glass ceiling. You probably have learned, just as I did, how once you hit a top in your business, you start going backward if you don't bust through. I reached a glass ceiling at the end of thinking only about myself and my comfort. You may have experienced the same thing in your business. If your goals are only about getting wealthy and living comfortably, you end up robbing the world of the gifts you have to share.

I believe there exists a natural and spiritual law that says, "The moment you start living only for your success is the day you start heading to ruin." We are born knowing this universal truth intuitively. This is why many people in the world instinctively choose to start a family—so we can put the well-being of another higher than ourselves. Through our spouse and children, we play a part in making the world better than how we found it.

Before you read this book, I want to frame your mindset first. The world needs you to get back on Google and succeed—not for your benefit, but the world's. For those of you who can build a business, you need to make it as large as possible to help as many people worldwide as you can. Don't settle for "enough." Instead, focus on transforming the world, and you will shoot right past "enough." You will obtain everything you want if you focus on helping as many other people as possible. The more people you help achieve their goals, the easier your dreams will be to achieve.

My Journey

When my mentor taught me how to use Google AdWords (the previous name of Google Ads) to build an online business empire in January 2009, I began a breakout year as an internet marketer.

After one month of using AdWords, I had my first profitable month as a business owner, making a little over one hundred dollars. I sat at my computer stunned, looking at the very first profit I had ever made online. It felt like an out-of-body experience. It took a few seconds to snap back and realize what I was seeing was real. Overwhelming emotions of joy and happiness began to take over my body, and I started shouting, "YEAH!!!!!!" and jumping up and down. As I was jumping for joy, I felt something warm on my cheeks, and when I touched my face to feel what it was, I noticed tears flowing down my face. I laughed uncontrollably.

My wife, Joni, came into the room to inquire about what was so funny. I looked at her with the biggest smile on my face and said, "Baby, we're going to Red Lobster tonight. And this time, we don't have to order off the kids' menu!"

My success didn't end there. It only got better. The following month, I made just under one thousand dollars, and the month after that, I made my first five figures.

In May 2009, I made over one thousand dollars in a single week for the first time. When I first saw the amount of money I made, I felt paralyzed by happiness. I must have stared at my account for an hour, counting and recounting all those zeroes. The sense of amazement that I had made all those sales in a single week was overwhelming. I almost felt guilty about how easy it was to make money now, especially considering how hard it was to even generate a single sale before. Until learning about Google AdWords, I wasted so many years trying to do SEO and link building to sell my affiliate and network marketing products. It was so hard to get any traction building a business that way. Now, I was making sales and real profit, and all I had to do was put up an ad and add some keywords to a campaign. It seemed surreal, like I was using some magic trick to print money online. But I wasn't. It was all real and completely legitimate.

At this point, my confidence was soaring. I was building up the traffic from Google slowly because the only money I had to pay for my ad spend was my savings from my job and reinvesting my profit. After my first five-figure week, I boldly went to my wife and began to give the most passionate sales pitch on why we should borrow money and put it toward Google ads.

"Look, honey," I said. "We can borrow ten thousand dollars from the bank and invest in Google Ads. I can make back twice that money, easily."

She was skeptical. After all, she was there to watch all my business failures up until this point. Google Ads may have seemed like just another gimmick that also wouldn't last. I didn't blame her for pushing back, but I was so convinced of the results I would get if I just had more money to pour into ads that she finally agreed to us getting a loan. When we ultimately got funded, the first thing I did was crank up the budget on my top two campaigns. The traffic exploded almost instantly. I hit the refresh button on my browser about one hundred times that day. The sales were rolling in, even faster than before.

This excitement and growth continued for five days, and at the end of the first week, I had made $9,480 after only spending a little over four thousand. Oh, man, the feeling! It felt like, for the first time in my life, I was able to exhale. The self-validation was indescribable. I was only sleeping three hours a day, but I woke up feeling better than ever.

We were going to make it, I thought. *More than that. We were going to make it big.*

I went to my mentor, Mark Hoverson, and showed him my success. He told me, "Make a landing page about it. People need to know what you know. You'll crush it then!"

So I did.

I wanted the world to know I had made it, and I wanted to teach them to do the same thing, too. I hired a professional website designer, a copywriter, and coder with the remaining six thousand dollars I borrowed. I then took the revenue from my best week and paid my Google invoice. I decided to take the left-over profit and invest all of it into Display Network traffic. I was nervous to invest the rest of my money into Google, but with my last gamble paying off, I felt a little unstoppable. I upped my bids on Google. This turned the traffic spigot on and the impressions came flooding in. Leads started pouring in. People from all walks of life were coming to my website, wondering what I was doing to change my life so drastically, so quickly. My name shot up the leaderboard in my affiliate company. Very few people had ever heard of me, so it came as a surprise that someone who wasn't considered a "leader" in the company jumped to the top of the leaderboard so quickly.

I wanted to show off my newly found success. After all, what's the sense of making money if you can't spend it, right?

I purchased a brand-new car. I went to the nearest new car dealership to my house and left the lot with a new Chrysler Sebring within 45 minutes of arriving. I bought my wife a 4-carat weighted diamond ring. Then, I took the entire family clothing shopping at the mall. Nothing was off limits that trip. Whatever my family liked, I purchased it. I borrowed money to pay for all of it, but I didn't care. I knew I could pay it back with my profits later.

Everything was going so great. Everything was finally "right" in my world...until "that" day.

The Day It All Came Crashing Down

One morning in mid-June, I woke up full of energy as usual and danced to my desk in my home office. I didn't need any coffee to get going those days; everything was so awesome. As I sat in front of my computer, all excited, I shook my mouse and waited for the screensaver to come up.

Just how much money has rolled in already from those changes I made last night?

I couldn't wait to see the numbers of clicks and conversions. My fingers hovered over my calculator, ready to compute my profit for the day. But something happened when I hit refresh that shook me to the core. There was a red bar across the top of my account.

Immediately, the blood drained from my face, and I began to feel cold. I had never seen a red bar in my account before, but my body instinctively knew that the red color meant, "Danger! Something is very wrong!"

Before I could search further, my eyes darted down the page to look at my campaign numbers. When I saw them, I felt like I lost consciousness for a few seconds.

Zero conversions, zero clicks, and zero impressions since last night.

When I finally snapped back to consciousness, my heart was beating loudly. My eyes went back up to the top of the screen.

Maybe I was misreading something. Perhaps this red bar was there to alert me to some Google problem on their end?

When I read the text in the red bar further, it stated something about my account I didn't know existed. It said my "Google AdWords account had been suspended for violating the terms and conditions." This was the first time I was even made aware that there were rules to advertising on Google.

Up until now, all I ever did was follow the advice of my mentors and leaders who were crushing it as internet marketers. They all claimed they were paying for marketing almost exclusively on Google, but none of them mentioned anything about Google having rules that could get you kicked off their site.

I began to go into a frantic panic. I thought of all the money I borrowed and what my wife's face would look like when I told her what had happened. We took a giant leap of faith in me starting this business, borrowing money, and running up the cost of my Google Ads invoice in hopes the revenue I made after would cover it. Also, I purchased the brand-new car, the ring, and all those clothes at the mall. I had spent tens of thousands of dollars in a very short time. I didn't want to say anything about it to my wife. At least until I got more information about what was going on.

The first step I took was to find out what in the world a "suspension" was. I did many Google searches and found out that other people had experienced the same thing. Very few people had any information about it, though, other than reporting that they had the same problem and also couldn't find out how to fix it. Well, after much frustration and searching, I went back into my AdWords account and tried to see if there was a solution to this.

I looked back at the red bar at the top of my screen. I noticed there was a little arrow at the end of the red bar I hadn't seen before. I clicked that little arrow, and it scrolled to another sentence that stated if I wanted to know more about the suspension, click the "Learn More" link. When I clicked, it took me to a page inside Google's Help Center that talked about suspensions, what they were, and why they do them. There was also a phone number to call if you had questions about it. I called that number, and I got an awesome woman on the phone who explained everything to me. As we talked, she explained that this has happened to many advertisers recently because Google increased enforcement of policies across the network.

I didn't even know they *had* policies.

She said my advertising violated Google's User Safety policy. I asked her if she could teach me how to fix the problem, and she said she didn't understand the guidelines well enough to tell me exactly how to fix it; however, she could get me in touch with her supervisor, who may be able to help. Eventually, after being passed on to a few people, I talked with someone in upper management (if you're surprised I actually talked to a real person at all, keep in mind that this happened way back in 2009, when Google support was much less structured and higher management levels were more accessible than they are today). This person was very friendly and took the time to teach me all about Google's ad policies, User Safety, and what changes I needed to make to my website to get my account reinstated. He then instructed me to learn more about their policies in Google's Policy Center (where Google discloses all their policies for advertising to the public), so I don't violate another policy while making changes.

Over the next week, I read as much as I could about policy, and for whatever reason, I had an affinity for this information. When I read it, it made sense to me. I actually got pretty excited about it. I began to think, "Wow, if other people are having the same problem, if I make these changes, I'll have a competitive edge in the marketplace."

I took what I learned in that week and made the necessary changes to my website. I had that manager review my website when I finished, and he said it was perfect. He then submitted my account for re-activation and said he would reach back out to me via email when he gets an answer from the Advertising Team about reinstatement. When he emailed me back, he told me my AdWords account has been un-suspended, and I will be receiving traffic again within twenty-four hours.

"Thank the Lord!" I shouted when I read his email. It felt like a hundred pounds of pressure lifted off my shoulders. That's when I finally told my wife what had happened and how I overcame it.

Boy, if looks could kill! She gave me the same look I got from my mom when I broke her china plate in the dining room and tried to cover it up.

After I finished telling her everything that happened, she sighed, shook her head, and said, "Honey, I'm not mad that this happened. I'm angrier you didn't trust me enough to tell me what you were going through. I believe in you, no matter what happens. So don't be afraid to tell me when things don't go as planned; that way, I can support you in any way I can.

Wow. I always knew my wife was special, but at that moment, I realized just how grateful I was to God for bringing her into my life. I was expecting to get an ear full, but what I got instead was a gift of encouragement and confidence to move forward with our business, unafraid of failure.

After this, I built and grew my affiliate business online using AdWords exclusively for website traffic. I stood out in the market because I was one of the only affiliates in my company still on Google. Everyone else kept getting kicked off for breaking policy rules.

Well, two months later, a gentleman reached out to me, who was also an affiliate marketer selling the same affiliate products I was. He had asked me if I had gotten suspended from Google AdWords recently, as well.

"Yes, I had, but I'm back up and running again."

He couldn't believe it. He had spoken to dozens of leaders, internet marketers, home business owners, and affiliates, and none of them had been able to get their AdWords account back up and running after getting suspended. I was the first one he'd heard of who had managed to do it. He then asked me if I could help him get back up and running, too.

I said, "Sure, but you're gonna have to make some significant changes to your website."

He said he was willing to do whatever it took at this point, because his business was on the verge of shutting down.

So, over the next couple weeks, I worked with him one-on-one to help make changes to his website. We then submitted his website, and Google approved his account. He was back up and running. He was in complete disbelief.

During the entire time that I was making the changes to his website, I explained what I was doing or why I was doing it and why Google wanted to see it done precisely that way. After Google reinstated his account, he said to me, "Dathen, what you're doing could change the landscape for internet marketers everywhere. Thousands of marketers are being suspended and kicked off Google every single day, and they don't understand what you understand."

He then asked if I would be willing to teach other marketers what I knew, if he got a group of them together to listen to me.

I didn't like the idea. Honestly, I was terrified to do it. I mean, I knew my business, and I learned how to make it Google compliant, but to tell a group of strangers from all different companies how to do it? I didn't know if I could help those people. I mean, what if what I did was a fluke? What if what I did only worked for our business model and not anyone else's? I was having a terrible case of "imposter syndrome" (feeling like a fake expert).

Well, he must have been a lot better at sales than I was, because he convinced me to do it even while I was trying to convince him I couldn't. To my surprise, the event was a smashing success. The group he put together loved it and found it extremely helpful. Most of them were able to make the proper changes to their advertising, and Google allowed them back on as well. Some didn't, but they didn't blame me for it because they told me they should never have promoted their products, to begin with. Turns out Google had their products on their "banned products" list.

I am forever grateful to that training group. By trusting me enough to let me into their businesses and allowing me to help fix their violations, I gained the confidence to start a brand-new Google compliance consulting firm and help other people.

That was in the fall of 2009. Fast forward to today, and I have helped hundreds of internet marketers and businesses fix their non-compliant websites and get back on Google again. As a result, many of them went on to make more money than they ever have before.

And this is why I'm writing this book. Over the last eleven years, I've seen a shift in the market that is troubling me. More and more marketers are moving away from opening a Google Ads account and trying other networks instead, like Facebook, Twitter, or Instagram. The mentors who teach them how to do paid marketing online are afraid of telling them to use Google Ads simply because they might get kicked off Google. This fear seems justified since Google likely also banned the mentors, but because of this, there appears to be an entire generation of internet marketers who have absolutely no experience with Google Ads, the single most significant source of quality website advertising traffic on the planet.

And this troubles me, because all of us O.G.s (Original Googlers) made our fortunes as an internet marketer using Google Ads without turning to Facebook or other smaller traffic sources. I like Facebook and other platforms, but the problem with Facebook, in my opinion, is that you have to keep up socially, and if you don't, the traffic may not last. On top of that, these alternative networks are starting to implement the same policies and enforcement measures that Google uses, due to the increased levels of fraud and scammers invading their networks.

So now the same marketers who couldn't keep up with Google policies are losing their traffic on Facebook as well—and this is a trend across the board on all the high traffic networks.

I designed this book to help you break the vicious cycle of creating a Google Ads account, running ads for a while, then getting banned. I started Google Compliance Secrets to keep your account from getting banned and show you the hidden ways elite marketers are getting rewarded from Google for promoting compliant ads. Doing this isn't some mystery that can't be solved. There's an exact blueprint every marketer can follow, and if you do, you will be able to access traffic that you couldn't when you were pushing noncompliant content.

For the most part, it doesn't matter what vertical you're in, as long as you aren't selling a banned product. There is a compliance blueprint that allows you to launch as many business verticals as you want. With this blueprint, you will be able to sell to an endless stream of people on Google and know that your traffic is going to be there the next morning, without a red bar of death in your account.

This is about your future. It is about creating a sustainable business model that will last through the times. This is about the employees that you've had to let go because you kept getting kicked off of Facebook and Twitter, and the other traffic sources were being squeezed more and more with little expansion left to get. This is about your family. You deserve stability in your business, and there is no more stable source of internet traffic than Google Ads. It is so powerful, and it is so consistent, that you can create ads and not have to change them for years because the traffic is that consistent and that good.

Keep an open mind as you go through each chapter of the book. There will be some challenging things that you've never learned before that you're going to have to tackle. Some of my advice may challenge some of the coaching and training you have received, but keep in mind that you are trying to make a huge transformation in your business. If you feel you could get to the next level without Google, then you wouldn't have picked up this book in the first place.

Aren't you tired of having to open up a new Facebook account every other week? Aren't you tired of Twitter banning your ads? Aren't you tired of Instagram taking down your post?

There's a solution. Get back on Google. Fix the problem at the core and create compliant advertising. This book will teach you how.

Through Google, you can finally reach the heights you know your business can achieve.

CHAPTER ONE

Chapter 1

Why People Get Banned From Google

Many people have experienced the pain of losing their Google Ads account overnight, or seeing all their ads disapproved due to some serious "AdWords violation." The most frustrating thing about this is that there isn't enough specific information about the violations for advertisers to know exactly what they did wrong or how to fix it. Because of this, Google Ads, for many, may seem like an elusive mythical creature.

When my account first got suspended, that's how I felt, as well.

However, I've since learned that Google Ads compliance isn't some mythical creature that can't be conquered or understood. I've now worked with hundreds of businesses and have found that most of them could undo their suspension through a few simple structural changes to their website—changes that may not have even have hurt their conversion rate.

It's not impossible to understand, and in many cases, people are only a few steps away from greatness. Let's take a look at some of the most common missteps.

Risky advertisers

Advertisers often get suspended because they are labeled a "risky advertiser." A risky advertiser is someone who disregards the safety of the users of their website, risks Google's brand reputation, or is doing business in a way that Google deems as having "unsafe business practices."

For many years, Google had very little enforcement of their policies. AdWords was a growing brand, and Google wanted to do very little to hinder its growth curve. But that all changed in 2009 when the FTC (Federal Trade Commission) warned Google to take action to protect their network against scammers, or else they will be held liable for their advertiser's business practices. At the time, scammers were advertising on Google AdWords freely because Google took no action against these scammers, even those who dared to use Google's actual brand name in their scam.

That year, the "Google Money Tree," "Google Pro," and "Google Treasure Chest" scams papered Google's ad network with promises of making people one hundred thousand dollars in six months if they used their free home business kit. To get the kit, people had to pay a nominal shipping fee with their credit card. Unsuspecting searchers thought Google had endorsed the product, and thousands of people who found their ad on Google paid the shipping cost for the kit, giving these scammers their credit card information. What occurred after can only be described as one of the most lucrative scams launched on Google in the last decade.

After people gave these scammers their credit cards, they began to charge their cards as many times as possible until their credit card company blocked the charges. Some people said the scammers charged them seventy dollars a month for several months after they called and cancelled their subscriptions. Many people lost hundreds of dollars for requesting this so-called "free" kit (Federal Trade Commission, Press Release, September 2012). FTC's warning was a wake-up call to Google that they better start enforcing policies or face significant repercussions.

After this, they began targeted enforcement on "make money" offers that violated network policy. Google apparently then thought they solved the problem, because they did very little to enforce their policies on other industries. That came back to haunt them.

In 2011, the FTC slapped Google with their first significant lawsuit for allowing illegal online pharmacies from Canada to advertise on AdWords with impunity. These unlawful online pharmacies hurt thousands of Americans by promoting fake, tainted, or illegal drugs to unsuspecting victims and taking millions of dollars from seniors. To avoid prosecution, Google settled with the justice department for five hundred million dollars and agreed that they would take concrete action to clean up and enforce their policies on its advertising network. This was when Google decided to start proactively finding risky advertisers on its network and getting rid of them.

Can you blame them? I mean, we are talking about half a billion dollars. This was the first real threat to their business's future, and they needed to correct it fast. Since this incident, Google has invested significant money into human and artificial intelligence technologies designed to detect high-risk advertisers on their network. Because of these investments, Google has the reputation of being the most regulated online advertising network—and the numbers would back this up. Since 2011, Google has banned, suspended, or disabled over twelve billion ads, websites, and advertisers from their network[1]. For this reason, it is essential to understand what Google considers "risky" so you can make any necessary adjustments so your advertising is as un-risky as possible.

The Risk Meter

To be allowed to run on Google is not about being perfect or about having zero risk. There's risk in everything you do in life. You don't need to have a perfect website. It's not about having perfect ads either, or perfect landing pages, or products that make no claims. What it is about is the risk you pose to the visitor, the risk to Google's brand reputation, and the risk to Google legally. There is an acceptable level of risk that Google's willing to accept from advertisers. This acceptable risk level is determined internally in Google by using what was explained to me by a Google policy specialist as a concept called "the risk meter."

The risk meter measures the amount of risk Google will tolerate. Think of it as a point system. For every risky thing you do, it adds a point of risk. Once you cross a certain threshold of points, you become too risky of an advertiser for Google to allow on their network. Your job is to understand where that line is for your business and make sure that your website, ads, and advertising stay below that line.

Some industries start with risk points because of the nature of the industry, such as with over-the-counter (OTC) drugs. Still,

---

1. Search Engine Land, Mar. 2012, Google Blog, Jan. 2013, Search Engine Journal, Jan. 2014, The Guardian, Feb 2015, Google Blog, Jan. 2016, Google Blog, Jan. 2017, Tech Crunch, Mar. 2018, Tech Crunch, Mar. 2019

almost all industries can be advertised on Google Ads successfully, even if they're riskier, as long as they understand the risk meter, promote within policy guidelines, and stay below the risk thresholds, which we will discuss next.

Lack of business transparency

What the risk meter for Google comes down to is a way to measure your business's transparency on your website. Business transparency refers to how much about your business you are willing to disclose. The vast majority of businesses that violate the safety of the environment on Google usually fail to be sufficiently transparent in three main areas:

First is the nature of your business. Although you understand your business, people on your website don't—unless you explicitly explain it to them. I have had advertisers come to me who were kicked off Google for violating Google's "Untrustworthy Promotions" policy for promoting fake news articles. Transparency of the business model is very closely tied to this violation. In the case of these advertisers, who were promoting fake news articles that had links to affiliate products, there weren't any details about the actual company who created the phony article, and many customers who wanted to contact the "news agency" were not able to do so. Examples like these fake news story promotions may create a trust issue between searchers and Google for allowing these advertisers to market with such horrible business practices.

The second way a business may fail to be sufficiently transparent is in how the business uses personal information. The majority of businesses want to use personal information to make money—in fact, if you boil down all business performed online, it is all basically exchanging personal information for commerce, in one form or another. Credit cards, lead forms, "contact us," downloaded content, or even checking account purchases are examples of how you exchange personal information with a business to get a product or service. As a business, If you're not upfront in disclosing what you're doing with people's information, it creates an unsafe environment for Google's users.

Many suspended businesses have trouble with personal information disclosure in one way or another. For example, one of the most common ways is when businesses offer something for free on their website in exchange for opting into a form. Typically, the marketer creates a desirable free offer for something the visitor wants and promises they will deliver the offer once they put their personal information, usually name and email, into a form and submit it. Only after they submit the personal information will they then receive access to the free offer. However, what the visitor often does not know is by filling out that form, they have become a lead for the business owner, and that business owner plans to market to them, via emails, texts, or phone calls, other paid services. What makes this particularly troublesome for Google is that the business owners didn't disclose that they also agreed to be marketed to when they submitted their personal information for that free offer. This action frustrates visitors and makes them less likely to click on ads on Google in the future, thus, reducing searcher's trust in Google itself. Ultimately, this leads to less ad revenue for Google and a loss of public confidence in their services, which hurt their long term growth.

The third way a business may fail to be sufficiently transparent is how its website interacts with people's computers. This policy's phrasing is somewhat outdated, as "computers" are much more than just a desktop or laptop today. We now have smartphones, two-way devices, tablets, smartwatches, apps, text messaging services, the "cloud," Fitbit, and the like, all of which we can use to communicate with potential customers and exchange personal information. A much more accurate description would be to reword this policy to say: "how your website or business interacts with people's *devices*."

There are entire categories of businesses that struggle with compliance in this area because they do not thoroughly disclose what they're going to be doing to people's devices to communicate with them and facilitate commerce. It may be completely innocent on your part, if you happen to be someone in such a category, but in the big picture of risk, some business categories are more susceptible to suspension than others because frequently they do not do a good job of disclosing everything they're going to be doing to communicate and facilitate commerce on a person's computer or device.

An example of one such business category is third-party remote tech support services. Third-party remote tech support services are computer technical service businesses whose primary services are fixing computer issues remotely. They are referred to as "third-party" because they are not the creators of the software or hardware but rather have services to repair potential damage to people's computers remotely. For example, if you have a Dell computer that won't correctly run and you contact Dell technical support, that would be considered "first-party," since Dell is the computer maker. However, if you contacted Geek Squad from Best Buy, since they didn't create the computer, they would be considered third-party.

One of the most significant issues with running a third-party remote tech support business is that you may need to access the customer's computer remotely, many times requiring a particular software program downloaded onto the customer's computer to do so. Since people have to forfeit their privacy and give access to strangers to receive this type of support, this industry comes with an inherently higher risk, even if they do everything above board. These businesses must walk a tighter rope with more disclosure than most to help all parties feel safe with their business practices. This is all because if the third party remote tech supporter was a scammer, they could do untold harm to a customer once they access their computer.

An easy way a legitimate third-party remote tech support company may get themselves in trouble with Google is to install software programs onto their customer's computer without permission and then leave the software programs installed on the computer after the repair. By leaving it on the customer's computer without authorization or properly disclosing why the program remains on their device, Google considers it spyware (spying software).

It is essential to take these three areas to heart when creating your website. They are the spirit of Google's internal evaluations for risk, and all subsequent assessments are based upon these three factors. If you want to establish a relationship with Google Ads where you're going to have a long advertising history, you have to be as transparent as you can on the nature of your business, how your business uses personal information, and what your business is doing to a client's device.

In summary, the process of being banned from Google is a function of the level of risk you pose to the Google user, Google's brand reputation, and Google legally. Google uses a "risk meter" in determining how risky it will be to them to allow you to run your ads on their network. A large part of evaluating that risk is based upon your business's level of transparency to the public. Transparency of business model, company, and product are three keys to keeping your risk score low. Within this, making sure you are transparent about the nature of your business, how you use personal information, and how your website or business interacts with people's devices will lay a strong foundation for transparency to Google. Take the time to do a layman's "gut reaction" evaluation of your website to see if your alarm bells go off by asking yourself the following:

1. Would you consider your marketing message potentially "risky?"
2. Could your marketing practices cause problems for you or Google?
3. Can people easily find business and product information about the business, or do you lack overall business transparency?

If you answered "Yes" to any of these, your site has the potential to be taken down by Google for risk. It is essential to learn the additional information in this book to strengthen your understanding of how to correct this higher risk level before making changes without formal knowledge of how to do so. If you have a business model that is inherently risky by nature, you will need to start with an above-the-line mental approach. Think of it as playing "mistake-free football," which is to say, don't play around with the gray area when your margin for error is small.

For example, are you selling assistance applying for governmental services, such as travel visas or address change services? If so, make sure you make it clear that you are not associated with the official source. This disclosure should come immediately, right at the top of your website. Is your affiliate marketing website pretending to be the parent company or merchant? Or did you adequately disclose that you are a separate company from the parent? Do you put disclosures in so fine a print no one can read it, to hide important facts? Evaluating your site to see if it lacks the necessary transparency, such as in the above examples, can help you catch Google compliance issues with your website in the creation stages before you are exposed to being thrown in Google jail. This evaluation, combined with the information in the next chapter, will help you decide if you need to change your product or business model entirely to be allowed to advertise on Google Ads.

CHAPTER TWO

Chapter 2

Who is Google Ads For?

I was at an internet marketing conference five years ago, which featured internet business titans and small internet entrepreneurs from over one hundred different industries. During this event's breakout sessions, I would sit toward the back and listen to people get up and vent their frustrations to the discussion leader. One after another, from affiliate marketers to supplement sellers, many of them griped and moaned about how Google kept shutting them down, no matter what they did. Inevitably, after venting their frustration, they would ultimately conclude that they simply had to move on to other networks.

This made me sad. I wanted to jump up and say, "That isn't true. Following the rules can be as simple as following this blueprint!"

But that wasn't how the leaders structured this conference. I didn't want to seem self-serving, since I sell compliance consulting services as a business model. It would have severely hurt my reputation in their eyes if I did that. So I watched quietly in the back.

However, my sadness turned to frustration when the discussion leaders in the breakout groups agreed with them, as if everything they were saying was right. They agreed and nodded in frustration themselves, giving the people in the group the impression that Google just "hates" them. As I listened, it became clear to me that the leaders in this conference must not have been taught the rules of Google Ads, since my clients (who were in the same verticals as these people) did not have the same experiences. In fact, after listening to what the leaders were saying they were doing and how they were promoting their businesses on Google, it was clear to me that many of them shouldn't have even opened an account in the first place. They desperately needed a basic understanding of who Google Ads is even for, and to structure their websites accordingly.

So, who is Google Ads for? Google Ads is for businesses that sell products and services.

Businesses. Not people.

There is a belief among some marketers that if you have a product or service or some idea to sell something, all you have to do is throw up a quick website or a short landing page, open up a Google Ads account, and run some ads to make money. But in Google's terms and conditions for advertising accounts, there is a very explicit statement about who is allowed to advertise on their network. It says that Google Ads is for businesses who sell products and services, not people who sell products and services (Google LLC Advertising Program Terms, 2020).

Google doesn't want people, on a whim, to open up an account and sell something. The reason why is because people who put up websites and sell stuff with no real business behind the website are very risky to Google. They have no known customer service and typically have little recourse for bad products. They tend to lack transparency and have poor follow-through. Overall, they are usually bad experiences for users and may hurt the Google brand very deeply.

Therefore, Google has decided not to allow just any "Joe Schmo" to jump on their platform, slap up a website, advertise, and make money. They only want proper businesses, so you must have the minimum standards to be considered an acceptable business model.

First, you must be a business that sells a product or service of value. This is subjective and can vary widely, but it should appear to the layman's eye that there is real value to a potential buyer. Second, when you create your website, you must create the image that you are a stable, sound proprietor who is serious about quality, sales, and service.

If you are a freelancer or contractor, you are probably wondering if Google will allow you to advertise. The answer is "Yes," because freelancers and contractors are considered sole proprietors; they are, by default, considered in business as self-employed. Freelancers and contractors need to disclose their name and services and how to contact them. Contact information is crucial to business success and is a sign of a legitimate business.

Legitimate businesses

Legitimate businesses are very proud that they are a business. They show it off like a brand-new European car. They don't hide anything, as it's a source of great pride. They're perfectly comfortable disclosing phone numbers, addresses, contact means, and communication channels, as doing so contributes to growth and sales.

Now, you don't need a government-registered business to be considered a legitimate business by Google ads. Just be a real business.

This requirement can be a little tricky if you work from home, as making your home address public may not be desirable. Also, you cannot use a PO Box or other mailing address services as your operational address. One technique home business owners use to avoid this privacy issue is to rent temporary commercial office space such as Regus or other short-term office space rental companies. We will discuss more ways around this problem in Chapter 7. There are solutions out there that can provide the transparency Google wants and still give you the privacy you deserve.

Summary

Google Ads is a platform for real businesses. Just because you have an excellent idea for a product doesn't mean you are ready to launch an ad campaign on the internet's most powerful advertising platform. A real business, in Google's eyes, is not based upon the number of employees, whether or not you have a government registered business, or if you have a storefront. According to Google, a real business is one that has a disclosed business name, a disclosed operational address, a disclosed phone number, and an obvious product or service, even if the product is simply information or content to consume. In short, you have a real business if you are willing to say, "I have a business, this is what we sell, and this is how you contact me" on your website.

As you can see, the bar is very low to qualify; however, many blackhat marketers and scammers neglect this basic rule on purpose in an attempt to elude law enforcement, trick Google's policy detection systems, or to hide from refunds and complaints. To not get lumped in with this crowd, take the time to create the necessary information to be considered a legitimate business while building your website.

A simple test

Ask yourself, "Am I proud of my business? Would I tell everyone I meet my business name, business address, and what I do?" If you answered "no" to any of these questions, then you may need to make changes to your business model and website first before opening a Google Ads account, because if you hide essential details such as these on your website, it will likely get you banned.

CHAPTER THREE

Chapter 3

Who Google Ads Isn't For

In the last chapter, you learned Google Ads is only for businesses. However, not all businesses are created equal. Some legitimate companies are still too risky to run ads on Google.

For example, one of my previous clients was the largest online seller of vaporizers in North America. At that time, vaporizers were narrowly an allowable product to be sold on Google Ads. By working with my agency for compliance, we were able to thread the policy line for vaporizers. He had a huge competitive advantage because his competitors couldn't keep up with the policy's nuances. Over time, US public and governmental sentiment about vaporizers began to change due to the increased use among underage children. As a result, Google began to put more and more restrictions on the vertical.

It was clear to me that the future of vaporizer sales was in trouble, and they could soon be banned from advertising on Google altogether. I told my client that they needed to get ahead of the market changes and create a different business model and marketing approach that would be less controversial. This way, they would be protected from any future heavy-handed policy decisions that may come, and they could continue to sell vaporizers on a large scale on Google.

So what did they do? Ignored me. Worse than ignoring me—they started selling candy-flavored vaporizer oils in addition to vaporizers, embracing the controversy. Their days were numbered, and before long, Google banned them. Today, no vaporizer industry can advertise on Google Ads. The risk is too significant for Google.

Don't promote a banned product or business model

It's essential to make sure you don't promote a banned business model. There aren't many that are outright banned; I have listed the most common banned business models below. Many of them are common sense why they aren't allowed. Outside of the below list, there are occasionally one-off verticals that get added to the list when a public outcry stops the vertical from advertising, or a law changes, forbidding it. Typically, merchant processors are the first to eliminate the transactions of newly banned verticals before Google adds them to the list. To keep up with the banned list changes, do a Google search for "Google Ads Policy Change Log" and "Google Ads Advertising Policies." It will list out all the current and upcoming policy changes.

Scammers

Did you know Google Ads is one of the larger targets for internet fraud as a private business? Scammers and identity thieves open Google Ads accounts with stolen credit cards, stolen personal information, made-up information, and all types of other mischievous actions, all to do nefarious things. It seems silly that I have to state the obvious—that if you are a scammer, you can't advertise on Google—but you would be surprised how many scammers contact my business each week, wanting help getting back on Google Ads.

The incredible thing about it is that they don't even think they are scammers. It happens so frequently, I'm no longer surprised at the level of delusion these people have when they tell me about their business. Some scammers have come to me promoting ridiculous things such as, "You Won a Free Cruise" ads, which include a spinning wheel graphic where everyone who chose to spin it was the winner of a free, 7 Day, all expenses paid Caribbean cruise. No one ever received a cruise ticket, but their email inbox would get flooded with spam, and their identities would be compromised. Another outrageous person once came to me promoting what they called, "Miracle Mud That Cures Diabetes." It is outrageous because there is no known cure for diabetes, only treatments that slow the progression of the disease, such as taking insulin shots or having bariatric surgery. Individuals who fall for scams like the diabetes scam often quit taking their medications in hope that they can be cured, but they end up worse than before they followed the scammer's advice because their disease has a rapid progression while off medication.

But I'll never forget one of the most outrageous scam advertisers who ever reached out to me for help. His name was Samer, and he ran a so-called "spiritual transformation" online business. For the nominal price of $999, he would pray for you and have your favorite dead celebrity temporarily possess you. He would sell temporary spiritual possessions of famous dead people such as Michael Jackson, Alexander the Great, Whitney Houston, or George Washington, and claimed the possession lasted for one full hour.

When Samer told me this, I thought, "He can't be serious, right?" But oh no, he was dead serious. He began to tell me stories of times he had this celebrity possess this client, and that celebrity possesses that client. Noticing I wasn't taking him seriously, he tried even harder to convince me—he explained that if I wasn't a great singer and I wanted to be, all he had to do was have the dead spirit of Whitney Houston possess me, and for an hour, I would sing like Whitney Houston. That's not all. He told me if I wanted to have a famous person's spirit permanently reside in me, all I needed to do was wire two back-to-back payments of $9,999 (conveniently just under the IRS regulated reporting amounts to track). He would seal their spirit in me for eternity! And, he said, that price is a total steal for customers, and he could charge even more if he wanted to—but he wanted to "make it affordable for people."

Needless to say, I turned down that one—but even if I did help him, Google would have kicked him off within hours.

Adult Industry

There was a time when pornography and other adult-oriented businesses were an allowable business model, but Google has decided to get out of allowing the adult industry to advertise. Whether it be films, toys, or adult sexual encounter dating sites, all levels of the sex industry are banned.

Illegal Drugs

Illegal drugs are country-specific, but a good rule of thumb is if it is a scheduled or illegal substance in the United States, it is typically banned in all countries by Google's policy team. Check your local country's laws on specific drugs outside of the United States, as some substances are legal in the United States but banned in other countries, and are thus not allowed to advertise on Google. A non-exhaustive list of prohibited drugs by Google Ads can be found on their website under the Help topic: Unapproved Pharmaceuticals and Supplements. Alternatively, go to www.legitscript.com to search for the product in question to see if it has been "red-flagged" (banned) in the country to plan to advertise in. You will want to do an exhaustive search here before deciding to promote your product on Google Ads.

Get Rich Quick Schemes

Get rich quick schemes are different from get rich quick scams. Schemes are strategies that make promises, either explicit (direct claim) or implied (suggested, but not explicitly claimed by the business), to obtain larger than average sums of money for little to no effort, low education, low risk, or low investment. Typically, get rich quick schemes are banned not because they don't have legitimate products and services, but because their promises of riches skyrocket the risk meter above the risk score threshold.

If you are a coach, consultant, or trainer who knows how to teach people how to create lots of revenue and profit margin, reposition how you present your offer. Do it in a way that doesn't seem like anyone and everyone who buys your product can or will achieve the highest levels of success. We will discuss this in great detail—including how you can promote potential larger than typical financial gain products, services, or education compliantly—in Chapter 8. For now, if you fall into this category, refrain from opening up a Google Ads account until you read this entire book and implement all the changes that apply to your business.

Get Thin Quick Schemes

Get thin quick schemes are similar to get rich quick schemes. They make promises, either explicit or implied, to obtain larger than the average user's experienced weight loss, fat loss, or health improvements, while claiming little to no effort or little diet and exercise modification is needed. Typically, they will promote the shortest time frames and the most significant weight losses experienced by users, without properly framing those results compared to the average user's experience.

Again, these schemes' business owners may indeed have legitimate products or services that help people; however, due to the nature of their promotion of such services or products, they artificially raise their risk score high above the accepted threshold.

If this sounds like you and you already created a Google Ads campaign, pause the campaign immediately, delete the active ads, read this entire book, and make edits to your promotion before reopening your ads so you don't get your website banned. Deleting your ads will signal Google's policy that you have identified a problem with your website, and you are stopping traffic until the problem is fixed. This can, in many cases, prevent a website suspension before it happens.

If you sell a supplement in any form as part of your weight loss plan, you must pay close attention to the next section as well.

Regulated Medical Ingredients and Drugs

One of the top reasons my supplement clients get in trouble with Google's policy team is because their supplement has a regulated medical ingredient in the supplement. There have been several cases where a client has a supplement with a variety of all-natural ingredients that also includes an active ingredient that is regulated. In that case, Google will hold the compliance of your supplement to the higher standard set of the regulated component, not to the lower standards of natural supplements. If you have checked to see if your product is on the banned list and it isn't, but Google continues to strike down your ads or website due to pharmaceutical claims, then you may be facing this violation due to one or more of your ingredients.

One example of this is a muscle-building supplement one of my clients couldn't get approved. He called Google over five times and spoke with five different people about what was wrong with his marketing or product, as he only used supplement ingredients in his product. Still, Google kept accusing him of selling a controlled drug. After contacting me, I ran his ingredients through Google's banned list and found the ingredient that was causing the problem. He had a supplement called DHEA in his product, which in many developed countries, although a supplement, is usually controlled as it has steroid-like effects on the body. This is an excellent example of how your intentions may be good, but a lack of understanding about policies may have you spinning your wheels trying to find the problem. Make sure you have a firm grasp of the level of regulation of each of your ingredients.

Now is an excellent time to pull out your ingredients list and compare it to www.legitscript.com and Google's Unapproved Pharmaceutical and Supplements list. If your product, in part or whole, is listed on either one, it doesn't necessarily mean it's the end of the road for your product. It may only mean the claims you are allowed to make are restricted. LegitScript is one of the best sources for learning what claims are allowable or disallowed on Google. Internet advertising platforms such as Google, Facebook, and Bing partner with companies like LegitScript to tell them what supplements are illegally promoted. They directly API into these companies' ad policy systems and update their internal banned or restricted list when they find new products to be regulated.

*Special note on Cannabidiol (CBD).

At the time of this book's publication, CBD has recently become more mainstream. CBD's health properties are starting to be more widely accepted by health experts, state laws, and the general public. Notwithstanding, it is still considered to be a banned supplement, not allowable either as a stand-alone supplement or as an additive ingredient to a supplement. Google's stance on this may change as the mainstream opinion of countries changes. Odds are, if it does get approved, more than likely allowable CBD products will be for topical use only, due to the increased potential for abuse if the product is ingestible.

Dangerous Weapons and Dangerous Weapon Accessories

In the United States, the right to keep and bear arms may be a chief cornerstone of the constitution—however, your right to sell them on Google Ads is not. Google will have nothing to do with dangerous weapons or accessories of any kind, nor will they allow you to teach people how to illegally use dangerous weapons, such as teaching people how to alter weapons to make them automatic, how to print 3-D guns, or how to make dangerous weapons undetectable by metal detectors, police dogs, or law enforcement.

This begs the question, "What does Google consider dangerous?" Think in terms of common sense for a child. A bullet is dangerous, but a scope to increase aiming accuracy is not. Dynamite is dangerous, but bullseye targets are not. Selling information on creating a 3-D printed gun is dangerous, but selling information on being a better shot during hunting season is not.

People or Businesses Involved in an FTC Lawsuit

Companies that are targets of federal investigations or federal lawsuits are a particular type of risk for Google. Although it is not guaranteed you will get banned, their general rule of thumb is to run away from advertisers with this problem as fast as possible, due to the FTC's known history to shift the blame to the bigger fish. The last thing Google wants is to get another fine from the FTC for you doing commerce on their platform because you have business practices that cause you to get sued by the government.

Summary

Google Ads is not for everyone. A little investigation upfront about your product or service can help you identify if you will end up getting suspended for advertising a restricted product or service. Altering your product or service presentation is required to go from out of compliance to within compliance. Make sure you check Google's updated Google Ads Policy Change Log, Google Ads Advertising Policies, and Unapproved Pharmaceuticals and Supplements page carefully to make sure your product, ingredients, or services aren't landing on this list. Also, use www.legitscript.com if you sell supplements or OTC medication and search for your product and ingredients. Ensure you don't have a banned ingredient or a content-restricted ingredient (meaning specific claims or product associations you cannot make). Bans and restrictions can vary by country widely, so pay close attention to which country has banned the product, as it may affect the approval of your website.

CHAPTER FOUR

Chapter 4

Innocent Mistakes Marketers Make That Get Them Banned Before Their First Click

The lightbulb should be starting to turn on about how vital a role business transparency plays in Google's eyes as it pertains to risk. Before moving forward, if you haven't already taken a long, hard look at your business and asked yourself the tough questions, go back and do so. If you skipped Chapters 1 and 2, go back and read those chapters. A lot of policy issues can be solved upfront, so I suggest you attempt to do so before moving forward.

However, I know how hard it is to evaluate yourself. I understand just how hard it is to look yourself in the mirror and be honest about your business's riskiness and how you promote it. I remember when my lightbulb first went off. It was like I was seeing the real advertising world for the first time. Until that point, my actions were all about "carbon copying" the professionals in my industry.

"What are they doing?" "What products are they selling?" "How are they writing ads?" "What promises are they making to get the sale?" I was singularly focused on copying what works without any self-awareness that what I may be copying may violate terms and conditions in Google's policy.

As I look back now, I'm somewhat embarrassed at what I was doing to make money on Google Ads. I was running ads that said stuff like, "I made $9,000 in one week using this simple system from home. You can too. I'll teach you how!" Nothing about this kind of advertising is transparent, but, at the time, I didn't see anything wrong with it whatsoever. Which brings us to our next topic: mistakes advertisers make that get them banned before they even put up their first ad.

Don't make rookie policy mistakes that can get you banned from Google Ads immediately. In the next few sections, I'm going to list out the most common mistakes that can get you tripped up before you even get a single click.

Offensive/Spammy Domain Names

It is a noisy world. In the internet marketing world, it is even noisier, because the barriers of entry to marketing are lower. The cost of advertising is cheap and affordable, and government regulation is lacking compared to traditional advertising. As a marketer, it is your job to break through that noise, grab your target audience's attention, and convince them to buy your product as quickly as possible. I understand the impulse to try to stand out from the crowd by buying a creative domain name that catches people's attention with offensive, spammy, disease-related, or incendiary words in them.

Buying spammy or offensive domain names like DiabetesCure. com, HackYourCheatingWifesPhone.com, or GuaranteedMillions.

com is tempting because of their obvious appeal to the emotional or physical problems people may be having. Back when I was an affiliate marketer, we would have mastermind calls about the latest techniques we are using to drive sales. We would brag about finding domain names like these, only to get them suspended the same month we uploaded them on Google.

Finding catchy domains are important and can make a difference in your marketing. Google understands this, and they do allow catchy, creative domain names, but when you go too far, Google will take immediate steps to make sure your domain name isn't exposed to the public on their network. Your domain name is one of the first things people see when they see ads on Google. If your domain name is offensive, exaggerated, misrepresents promises, or are spammy ("clickbait") in nature, you increase the risk to Google exponentially.

This is why Google is so aggressive in policing Ads. With domain names and ads, you can negatively influence searchers' view of Google's network without them ever clicking to go to your website. With this type of public exposure, they prefer not to do business with spammy domain names.

Website Hosting Mistakes

"Make our domain name private so no one can know who we are," and "Let's have one name for our website hosting, but another name on our website as our business name, so the real company stays private," and even worse, "Let's have a PPC Management company buy and host our domain name so no one can know just who is behind this website" are all scenarios I have heard from marketers who want to stay anonymous throughout their website process. They may have good intentions for not wanting their information disclosed, but the result may be a banned account.

The reason: transparency. You can't escape it. Business transparency is a core fundamental to Google Ads compliance, and any marketer who tries to hide details and gets caught is going down. I get pushback all the time from affiliate marketers about private hosting. They say things like, "I want it private so my competitors don't know what I'm doing to be a super affiliate," or, "I don't want an Alexa ranking (ranks how popular your site is), so people can copy me," or, "Every large company makes their domain name private to protect trade secrets," or worse yet, "My partner was banned from Google a while back, and I don't want it to trace back to me."

These may be legitimate reasons to hide your hosting website information; however, look at it from Google's perspective.

Google has kicked off millions of affiliate marketers for policy violations when they try to open new accounts with a new website and fresh content. They get private hosting to hide various billing and ownership details, so they don't make public who is behind the company. These items are red flags that lead Google's policy team and the Google policy bot to think this is a previously banned advertiser trying to circumvent their detection systems to get back on behind Google's back.

Even if you are making your website hosting private for legitimate reasons, to Google, you may seem like a banned advertiser trying to get back on Google Ads. This is especially true if you are marketing in a risky vertical and your content looks familiar to other content they have banned before. Thus, you might get suspended before you even run an ad.

As frustrating as this situation may be for you, a simple solution is to make sure your hosting ownership information matches the company billing. Matching these two up and allowing this information to be public will give Google the transparency it needs to keep your risk score down.

One Page Websites

Wow, do one-page websites convert! Out of all the A/B website split tests (performance improvement tests where we test something new in our marketing against our existing marketing) I have run as a marketer, one-page websites perform the absolute best. It isn't even close. The best example of this I've seen was with a split test I did to test if a two page, two step advertorial would increase sales over my one step, one page advertorial. At the time, my one page advertorial was converting at 5%, which was considered good. However, I needed it to convert at 8% because I couldn't add a second product to purchase on my website due to the parent affiliate company's rules. My thinking at the time was that a visitor would buy more if they trusted me more. The way I thought I could increase trust was to add a second page of information all about my product and reserve the first page for talking about the problem. Currently, I was giving information on both on the one page, but I decided to break it up in two pages. The sales rate of this new two page website process dropped the sales rate from 5% of visitors down to 0.34%, a whopping 93% drop in sales rate! This is the most severe drop in sales rate I have seen to date for a multipage website, but other marketers say they see the same pattern of sales rate drops every time they add more than one page to their website.

On the flip side, they have also produced more credit card chargebacks (forced refunds initiated by your credit card or bank), refund requests by customers, and complaints than any other website strategy.

I get it; they work. I mean, they work crazy well. However, the lack of business transparency of a one-page website is substantial due to the limits of information you can place onto one page of a website. Also, you may offend many of your visitors.

"What do you mean I may offend my site visitors by having a one-page website?" you might ask.

Well, society is generally broken up into two types of consumers:

1. researcher buyers, and
2. impulsive buyers.

Although everyone has a little of both in them, we tend to lean toward one or the other naturally. The bulk of buyers are researchers. Reading this book is a researcher trait. The fact that you are reading this book proves it, because educating yourself about Google Ads compliance requires patience. The majority of society leans toward researching a purchase more cautiously before buying, taking more time weighing the pros and cons to ensure the investment will have the desired result. Researchers prefer informative reviews, referrals, details about the product, and pros and cons. They take their time listening and reading, and when they commit to the purchase, they rarely have buyer's remorse, even if the product doesn't meet the expected need. In a perfect world, you would only sell to these people. They are committed purchasers and tend to have a higher lifetime value for your business if your product meets expectations.

However, marketers can get frustrated focusing only on them, because the buying cycle may take a while. Giving these people information to research means they may take longer to get comfortable with the purchase. This can be stressful on a business owner because they typically invest their money first, then get a return later, and if that "later" takes too long, then a business could have cash flow issues. Although a researcher's lifetime value tends to be higher, marketers are typically taught to emphasize the velocity of money (the speed at which money spent returns back to you so you can reinvest it). Since the velocity of money may be more important to them, they tend to rely more on business from the *other* side of the population: the impulse buyer, who makes much quicker purchasing decisions.

Impulsive-leaning shoppers love headlines and hard-hitting copy. They respond to grand promises and easy purchase paths. They don't like to be overwhelmed with a lot of information because it is hard for them to focus on what is essential to know, as they are more easily distracted. Quite simply, they provide fast money. We have all been impulse buyers at one time or another. Have you ever thrown a candy bar into your cart last minute at the grocery store? Impulse buying in action.

However, what marketers love about them is tied deeply to what they hate about them: buyer's remorse. Impulsive buyers make up the vast majority of the chargebacks businesses experience. They don't read disclaimers or terms and conditions of the sale. They tend to opt-in above the fold, so they didn't even see an auto-billing feature to get that low price. They get anxious when you put urgency on the page with a timer, and they purchase fast, without even reading how the program works.

These are the people who make working in customer service so awful. Impulsive-leaning buyers are more likely to be agitated people on the other end of the phone line, demanding a refund even though they aren't eligible according to the terms they agreed upon but didn't read. You see, that one-page website "attracts" the impulsive buyer, but repels the research buyer, so much so that many researchers get offended and go onto forums and tell the whole world how much of a "scam" you are. In my experience, many of the researchers who buy from a one-page website are other marketers, who either want to funnel hack you (copy your marketing or research what you are doing) or want your product's sales price but are forced to go through your one-page website to get the massive discount.

Another, more direct issue with one-page websites is that Google employees tend to be researcher-leaning people. To them, a one-page website looks entirely insufficient to deliver all the transparency a business would require to be safe for users. This is why one-page websites tend to be disabled from receiving traffic quickly once you create an ad to send traffic to one.

In Chapters 9 and 10, we will discuss creating a simple landing page that urges visitors to quick purchases and Google compliance. For now, if you plan to launch a one-page website on Google Ads, scrap that plan and learn how to build a proper website that policy will approve from the information in this book.

Using Previously Banned Domain Names

"Dathen, I don't understand what I did wrong," he said. "I just created this business a month ago. It's never been on Google before, no one could have complained, I'm not doing anything illegal...I did nothing wrong!"

This is a conversation I had with an affiliate in the health and wellness vertical. He had built a multimillion-dollar affiliate business model with another website using Clickbank as a medium; however, his new website kept getting disapproved by Google every time he created an ad. Google wouldn't allow him to run ads no matter what the ad said.

"Show me your website and what you have been doing," I asked.

He was a legitimate business. Unlike the previous warnings in Chapter 1 and Chapter 2, he, from the beginning, ran a business he could be proud of. But despite that, he couldn't stop Google from slapping him down every time he tried to put up an ad.

Upon further investigation, we learned he had made an unforeseen mistake. He purchased a domain name that had previously been banned by Google when it was owned by someone else. By trying to use that same domain name in his account, Google assumed he was the previously banned owner trying to circumvent their policy by opening a new account and using a new company name. After quite a bit of back and forth with a Google specialist and submitting numerous support documents proving he recently purchased this domain name, they finally let him advertise freely.

What sucks about this mistake is that you typically won't know if you have purchased a previously suspended website. Domain names get recycled all the time. The last thing you want to have happen is to find the perfect domain name, put your new content on it, upload it into Google Ads, and one hour later get the "red bar of death" across your screen saying your "Google Ads account has been suspended for violating our Circumventing Systems policy," without any knowledge of how you could have violated this policy in the first place.

Take heed to avoid this mistake. The only way to know for sure a domain name hasn't been used on Google Ads in the past is to ask a Google account representative to check if there is any history in the system for your domain name. Unfortunately, not all people will get assigned a Google account representative, so this may not be an option for you. Otherwise, I suggest not using a domain name if it has indexing history, to be on the safe side. A great tool to determine if a website has indexing history is to use the Wayback Machine, archived at www.web.archive.org. Run the domain name you plan to use for Google Ads through their free search tool and see what indexing history shows. I usually click on the oldest record, a middle record, and a recent record in the last twelve months. Ideally, you will see nothing or only parked domain history.

If you find a website you love but has indexing history of a business, and you want that domain name, you have a tough choice to make. You may try to proactively reach out to Google and let them know you have purchased a domain that may have had Google Ads history in the past, but let them know that you are the new owner of the site and the content will be completely different. This strategy has worked once for me in the past, but since it has only worked once, I don't have a proven track record that this will consistently work. With that said, it's always safer to buy a domain name in which you are the only recorded owner of that website.

Opening A Google Ads Account Before Your Website Is Compliant

I feel terrible for the advertiser that makes this mistake. Google has changed its new account creation process dozens of times. This warning is relatively new, because a few versions ago, Google started requiring you to put your domain name into the account before creating the account entirely. As a result, marketers who don't know any better put their domain name into the system to complete the account opening process, thinking they aren't running ads yet anyway, so what does it matter? Later, they return to the new account only to learn they have been suspended because their website wasn't compliant when they put it in.

Google tends to suspend accounts the most when they first open. Google tends to catch most of the bad actors in the beginning stages of an account, so they overreact to new accounts formed. That is why I recommend not opening a Google Ads account until you are one hundred percent ready to run an ad.

Using Prepaid/Virtual Credit Cards

Using prepaid and virtual credit cards is more of an international standard, not a United States standard. It is rather unusual to run across one of them here in the United States. From Google's perspective, only scammers use prepaid or virtual credit cards. I'm not sure why they have this perspective, but I haven't seen an account using a prepaid or virtual credit card approved for traffic in the last seven years. If you are international, you are better off using the checking account option than a prepaid or virtual credit card.

Opening Google Ads Account With Virtual Phone Numbers

Plain and simple: Google Ads does not accept virtual phone numbers to verify Google Ads accounts. Period. You can either use a hard landline or a real cell phone with a SIM card. Since I'm talking to marketers, I have to be extra clear here: no, you cannot use a second phone number on your phone. Get a cheap flip phone with a SIM card if you have to, and use it to verify your Google Ads account. It is all about transparency. For some reason, virtual phone numbers aren't as verifiable as regular phones. I don't know the exact reason why, but I do know that Google has a hard time verifying accounts with them, so they have decided not to accept them at all.

Linking To Banned Websites

Google holds you, the advertiser, directly responsible for whatever you link to or put in your Google Ads account. A common practice for affiliate marketers is to link to the parent company's affiliate link, but that can lead to problems.

Let's say your affiliate link is www.CancerCure.com/affiliate-marketerid and that this landing page is 100% compliant. However, the parent company's root domain, www.CancerCure.com was banned from Google Ads for promoting miracle cures. In this case, unfortunately, you may get banned, but they will certainly disallow the website link. Even if your website is compliant and not promoting a miracle cure, if the website you link to is, Google will hold you responsible for exposing their users to a banned website that is promoting noncompliant content and may suspend you, as well.

This rule carries a hefty penalty. It's rather harsh—because how would an affiliate marketer know the parent company's website is banned? Like I said in Chapter 1, many websites are suspended for the littlest things that could be avoided if they only knew about them, and this is one of those things you need to know before you upload an affiliate website into your account. The worst part about this violation is that Google gives you no grace or flexibility. Once you put the parent company website into your Google Ads account, you can't get your site or ad unbanned until the parent company makes their website compliant, which rarely happens. If you have made this mistake, you need to learn from this experience and avoid it for your future companies because this company's ability to advertise will be permanently linked to that noncompliant website.

Giving previously banned advertisers access to your Google Ads account

Once someone is suspended or banned from Google Ads, it is like they have an infectious disease that transmits to every Google Ads account they touch, forever. If you have an employee who has been banned from Google Ads in the past and didn't get it cleaned up, keep them away from accessing any computer associated with your Google Ads account. They are toxic people, as it pertains to Google Ads, leaving their "suspension germs" on every computer they touch. Let that person know they can't be associated with the Google Ads account in any way. They can't check their emails from that banned account on your company computers, they can't use the same server or IP address as the people who use Google Ads—heck, you may want to move them to another building just for good measure.

I think this part of Google is the most unfair. One accidental login to an email account associated with a banned account on a computer used to manage your Google Ads account can take down a perfectly good Google Ads account. Hopefully, in the future, they will become more lenient on this policy.

Getting Unbanned

I have helped people get their original Google Ads accounts unbanned through the years, but I will tell you that it isn't easy. Google treats people who were suspended in the past far worse than people who get banned today. Yes, it is discrimination, but since they are a private company and you violated their policy, they have the right to do whatever they want. I wish it were fairer and more equitable, but to avoid this mistake, you have to tell everyone with a suspension history that they can't be involved in the Google Ads account at all.

Summary

Internet marketers who have a history of getting banned from Google Ads tend to make many critical mistakes that lead to a suspension before uploading a single ad. This can guarantee the demise of an account before it gets a single impression. Study the list above of common mistakes and thoroughly check your website and hosting. Ask employees about their Google Ads history and double-check outbound links to make sure you currently aren't violating any of the above guidelines. If so, take immediate corrective action to avoid an account suspension.

CHAPTER FIVE

Chapter 5

Understanding the Google Ads Policy Team

Your mindset should be transforming, your marketing lenses you usually used to build a website should be changing. Hopefully this book should be putting into focus the things about your business that have prevented you from being able to keep your account unbanned and undamaged.

However, let me be clear: although I am speaking about compliance policies as if they are straightforward, clear, and an objective set of rules, in truth, it comes down to the people who are in charge of enforcing those set rules.

Let's meet those enforcers.

Meet the Google Ads Police: The Google Ads Policy Team.

The Google Ads Policy Team is a collection of people, complicated enforcement tools, software, and legal departments whose sole purpose is to pull over speeding advertisers and take them to jail (figuratively speaking). This group of Ivy Leaguers are trained to take down all violators of the most holy Google Ads Terms and Conditions, the rules you agreed to when you opened a Google Ads account.

If someone from Google is reading this right now, they are probably getting a little upset at me for making them seem like a religious cult. Sure, I may be using a bit of hyperbole here, but honestly, they are true believers in the Google Code. They believe they are keeping the world safe from evildoers (AKA internet marketers) who are abusing their most holy ad network and spreading chaos and destruction across the globe.

Their devotion and admiration of Google's Ad Policies are commendable, and their dedication is why they enforce them so aggressively. The engineers who coded their policy detection systems are meticulous, and their spyware digs deep into an advertiser's personal information and business. In my opinion, if Capitol Hill or the attorney general understood the complicated and intrusive tools used to investigate you by Google, they would drag them into court immediately, citing violations of the privacy granted us by the constitution.

I am laying it out like this because I want you to understand the difference between the policy's exact letter and the spirit of the policy that Google Ads has created. That difference is the way these true believers see the world. They are the gatekeepers. They hold all the keys to the whitelisting of your website. Sooner or later, you will have to confront one of them, and yelling and screaming won't get it done. You need to "understand" their mission, how their bureaucracy is structured, how to navigate to policy specialists, and ultimately how to use their policies in your favor.

Policy Team Mission

The Google Ads Policy Team's mission reads as follows:

"We want to support a healthy digital advertising ecosystem—one that is trustworthy and transparent and works for users, advertisers, and publishers...These policies are designed not only to abide by laws but also to ensure a safe and positive experience for our users. This means that our policies prohibit some content that we believe to be harmful to users and the overall advertising ecosystem." ("Google Advertising Policies Center", 2020)

Sounds lovely, right? In theory, if this is what they do, then this book wouldn't even need to be written, as no legitimate marketers would suffer the unbending wrath of the Advertising Team's enforcement tools. However, the way this mission has been interpreted and enforced by the employees of Google through their training is more like, "search and destroy advertisers we don't like."

The employees on the Google Ads Policy Team aren't salespeople. They don't have hard, bottom-line contributing metrics to show on their annual promotion reviews. I was having a conversation with a Google sales rep who had left Google and he was telling me about his experience working there. In our conversation, one of the topics we discussed was about the Google Policy Team. I asked him why the policy team's interpretation of rules has expanded beyond the spirit of the policy. He began to enlighten me on how the promotion process works today within the policy team versus how it used to work. He said policy team members mainly had to show their worth in the past with side projects outside of their policy working hours, making it very difficult to move up the corporate ladder. So, to differentiate themselves so they can move up the corporate ladder faster, they have redefined advertisers who have websites that have violated their rules as "bad actors." In the past, this label of "bad actors" was only reserved for the most egregious advertisers (scammers and businesses violating the law). By labeling most advertisers who violated policy as bad actors who destroy the peace and harmony of Google's online ecosystem, they have as a result created a hostile environment that seeks to "crack down" on unsuspecting advertisers, most of whom have only made honest mistakes.

They disable ads, websites, or accounts in the name of justice and equity, making the relationship adversarial between advertisers and Google when they should be working together. This has allowed its employees to show contributions to Google's brand in the way of the number of policy enforcements they have on record, so they can receive promotions and move up the corporate ladder easier and quicker. These people add a lot of "subjectivity" to the process of being Google Ads compliant, as Google empowers these individuals to interpret the policy as they see fit, as long as they in good faith are acting in Google's best interest.

I am telling you this so you can understand why violations are so challenging to get overturned. Although they have a front line, reactive support team you can speak to on the phone, that support you receive can be contrary to the "internal" mission. The Google policy enforcement teams are cops and judges, not defense attorneys or social workers. They are not your advocate, although their mission states otherwise. They post each year proudly just how many "bad actors" they "banned" or ads they took down that year. It is like a badge of honor to them, as if destroying accounts, businesses, and employees' lives is something to be proud of. For example, Sridhar Ramaswamy, Google's Senior VP of Engineering, wrote:

"In 2011, advertisers submitted billions of ads to Google, and of those, we disabled more than 130 million ads. And our systems continue to improve – in fact, in 2011 we reduced the percentage of bad ads by more than 50% compared with 2010." He continues by saying, "We're also catching the vast majority of these scam ads before they ever appear on Google or on any of our partner networks."

And if he left any doubt about how he feels about these 130 million advertiser's ads, he tops his comments off by adding, "We must remain vigilant because scammers will always try to find new ways to abuse our systems," he said. "Given the number of searches on Google and the number of legitimate businesses who rely on this system to reach users, our work to remove bad ads must be precise and at scale." ("Google Public Policy Blog", March 2012)

Over the last eight years, The Google Ads Policy Team has banned and removed over *twelve billion* ads and advertisers from their network. Think about all the businesses that may have been harmed or destroyed by losing the traffic associated with twelve billion ads, websites, and accounts.

You have to learn how to deal with these people to get your way, or you may fall victim to their overzealous flagging of ads, websites, and accounts for violations of policy. If you are going to do all this work to make your website compliant with their policies, you need to know how to protect it against overzealous policy enforcement.

Advertising Team vs. Google Ads Policy Team

One of the first steps is to understand how the policy team is broken down. To call them The Google As Policy Team as if they are one "team" can be misleading. I know they want to simplify things for people, but this leads to an inadequate understanding of how to fix policy problems when they arise.

In actuality, *two* primary teams are responsible for policing advertisers: The Advertising Team and The Google Ads Policy Team. They perform different functions but work together to enforce policy and support advertisers. The Policy Team gives speeding tickets, warnings, and prosecutes advertisers in the court of the Advertising Team law. The Advertising Team are the judges, and they decide whether or not to suspend accounts.

This knowledge will help you direct your energy to the right department when you have policy issues with Google. Advertisers often argue with the Google Ads Policy team when it was the Advertising Team that made the suspension decision. You need to understand which team has a problem with you to craft your responses and get the results you want.

For example, if your Google Ads account was suspended for violating the Terms and Conditions, this is an Advertising Team issue. Your business model or company information triggered a high-risk assessment that went to the Advertising Team. An individual on that team decided the threat was significant enough to warrant a suspension. Suspensions from the Advertising Team may not be because you violated a specific policy, per se. They are "risk" suspensions—they don't want to allow you to advertise on their platform because the risk outweighs the rewards.

A classic case that illustrates this is Wikipedia. As you probably know, Wikipedia at one time was the number one website to get user-generated, trusted information. Part of the reason they rose to stardom was the amount of Google Ads advertising they were doing at the time. However, a law was passed concerning copyrights that directly affected the user-generated content on Wikipedia. As a result, Google Ads decided the "risk" of having Wikipedia use Google

Ads to market their platform was too great, and outweighed the reward of their ad spend due to the legal complications. So the Advertising Team suspended Wikipedia. Wikipedia didn't specifically violate a policy; they just became too big of a risk.

You will know you are dealing with The Advertising Team when they tell you that you have to fill out a form, and support can't help you any other way. Also, they may say only the respondents to that form can communicate with you. If you are facing a suspension, once you have made your entire website compliant, focus your appeal more on the changes you made to your website for business transparency and product transparency. Relate all these changes to their policies and how all of these changes make your account, ads, and website a low risk to have on their network. This is highly subjective, as you can see.

Either the red bar in your account, an email you received, or reactive support itself will tell you the specific policy the Advertising Team is citing as their reason for the Terms and Conditions suspension. If they don't, I have found breaking down how I am not violating the Untrustworthy Promotions Policy (often referred to as the "unacceptable business practices" violations) line by line with supporting evidence has yielded the most success. How you would detail this is based upon your business model.

Let's use an example of a dog breeder client. This dog breeder had breeding practices that did not sit well with third party organizations like Peta. Although this breeder was following the law, this organization had a different opinion of what more he should be doing as a breeder of dogs. He didn't comply with their request, so they reported his behavior to Google in the hopes that they would take his ads down. This breeder got a suspension from the Advertising Team for violating Terms and Conditions. Although they didn't cite the actual policy they are referring to, typically, this scenario falls under Untrustworthy Promotions, since this policy deals the most with transparency, credibility, and safety. I had this breeder respond with their compliance to the law with supporting verbal and physical evidence.

There was a line in this policy I helped him attack aggressively in a crafted response with credible evidence that he did not violate this policy. It read: "False advertising of services that could endanger a user's health, life, or safety. Pretending to provide critical services that result in a delay to the user receiving treatment or medical help." This line has a broad application that can be interpreted and applied to many areas. In the dog breeder's case, Peta may have said that the breeder is misleading buyers into thinking his process is humane, when it isn't. The owner had to show that his breeding approach is compassionate using testimonials, showing their breeding process, including pictures of the kennel, and showing that the dogs can roam outside for "free time," as well as a few other private business details. This counterevidence was what Google needed to unsuspend this advertiser. After two weeks, Google sent him an email saying they had "good news" that his Google Ads account could run ads.

The Google Ads Policy Team is different, both in the magnitude of their power and their responsibilities. The Google Ads Policy Team is broken up into three policing areas: the publisher side, the third-party side, and the advertiser side.

Publishers are owners of websites that host Google Adsense ads (ads on a website) on their site. These individuals create valuable content for internet visitors to consume; then, they strategically reserve space on each of their website pages for Google to place ads from advertisers on their website.

Google will share the revenue of the click cost charged to an advertiser with the publishers. When an advertiser creates ads and places them on Google Display Network, those ads will show up on websites, and publishers own those websites. Because of the importance of publishers to Google, Google gives successful publishers a great deal of power to control what ads the publisher will allow on their website. Large publishers have a tremendous number of staff whose whole job is to look at their website's analytics (website traffic that is coming in, what ads are showing up on their site, and performance of that traffic and ads) to determine how profitable each ad has been for them, which ads cause the highest bounce rate (people who exit the website quickly because they don't like what they see), and which ads are potentially harmful to their visitor base.

Suppose a publisher finds an ad being served (shown) on their website, and it is noncompliant. In that case, they can immediately flag and report the ad to the Google Ads Policy team from inside their Google Adsense publisher account at the click of a button. This report will trigger a manual review of the ads from the Google Ads Policy Team. Google will then review the ads and websites to determine if they are in violation, and if they are, they will take punitive action. The publisher has the power to disallow your ads from showing on their website as well. This power can work as a suspension, but only at the website level.

The third-party side of the Google Ads Policy Team fields third party complaints. A great deal of policy enforcement comes from third party organizations and entities logging complaints, such as the BBB, trustinads, FTC, LegitScript, user complaints, and competitor complaints. These third parties often have access to information about the ads or website the Google bots cannot detect. As a result, the information reported by individuals and third parties is invaluable to Google's policy enforcement. They play a significant role in catching violations marketers think they have hidden from Google's view, such as in their email broadcasts or behind membership areas and upsell (additional product sales offers once the first offer is purchased) funnels. An important thing to understand is just because you are currently getting away with noncompliant advertising because the Google Ads Policy Team can't detect the violations with their bots, doesn't mean you won't get caught eventually.

I had a client selling weight loss supplements, and we did a lot of work to make their website and upsells Google complaint to get approved. Well, he did get approved and ran issue-free for eight months. In the ninth month, he woke up to the "red bar of death" (account suspension notice in a Google Ads account). Google suspended him for a "Circumventing Systems" policy violation (a severe violation that means Google caught him trying to trick their policy violation detection systems). He called me, furious about his suspension. He said had hired me to make sure this didn't happen, and he claimed he didn't change anything about his website in the last eight months.

So I went to work researching the source of this suspension, thinking it was a false flag by Google and seeing what evidence I could gather to get the suspension overturned. During one of my chats with reactive support, a policy specialist made me aware that they can't share the details of the circumventing with me, but what she could tell me gave me all the information I needed to know that the violation was accurate.

What the specialist said was, "We have more than one way of detecting circumventing. We use information and tools outside of Google Ads to gather information about an advertiser's marketing practices." She then went on to explain something rather peculiar. She said, "Remember, we are Google and have access to a vast amount of information that is indexed (website results in a Google search)." When she said it, it sounded like she was smirking, as if to say, "I can't tell you directly, but read between the lines."

That's when it hit me. Google was pulling up any information indexed! Forums, review sites, and your competitors may be talking about what you are selling. Also, other pages on your website may be indexed, and although they may not be reached by clicking through the sales process from your ad, they may be accessible at the click of a button to Google, since they own Google Search.

Armed with this new understanding of Google's ability to find information not easily found on your website, I researched how to view this indexed website content that I couldn't see by clicking an ad. I learned about a search function in Google called "site:" [sight-*colon*]. A "site:" search can be performed by anyone by simply opening up a Google Search bar, typing "site: the website name," then pressing "enter." A site: search would pull up all the links indexed to that site, just like they were typical search results.

I did a site: search on my client's website and saw a bunch of pages I never knew about that he was using, many of which were noncompliant. I needed to confront my client more about his claim that he "hasn't changed anything in the last eight months." I called him and asked him if he had any noncompliant advertising at all, regardless of if it was directly on their website or not. He said he did, but it was in his autoresponder series (automated email broadcasts) and wasn't directly accessible on the website, except through email. He said he thought Google couldn't see the noncompliant copy, that only people coming from emails could see it. He said he never thought Google would find out if it wasn't directly accessible from the homepage or landing page on his website. He apologized to me for blaming me.

Because of this experience, I prefer my clients not even email noncompliant information, as Google may decide to go on your list to see what happens.

The Google Ads Policy Team on the *advertiser* side is mostly an automated detection system, with strategic human support. They are working toward full automation, but they are not there yet. That said, today, most humans on the policy team are on the "reactive" support side.

The standard process with this team's policing of advertisers is this: the Google bot flags ads, websites, and accounts for potential policy violations in Google's system. The bot requests a manual review by a policy specialist to take a second look, then the specialist will review to confirm or overturn, if it is a false flag. While the policy team is relatively automated, unless it is an extreme situation or a brand new account opened, only humans (on the Advertising team) can suspend accounts. That may change in the future, as their artificial intelligence (AI) software policy bots continue to develop.

They can disapprove ads, disable websites, disable keywords, and such, but in general, they can't suspend a mature account (one that is not newly created). You know you are dealing with the Google Ads Policy Team rather than the Advertising Team because they always point to a particular Policy Center topic that is "flagged" in their system. In contrast, the Advertising Team typically refers to the vague terms and conditions.

The makeup of the Google Ads policy team is complex and vast. You have front-line reactive support (people who answer the phone or chat), managers of support, policy specialists, managers of policy specialists, technical support, policy writers, policy coders, and so forth. To make it more complicated, they have different teams *within* specific policies themselves, i.e., there is one team that handles misrepresentation and a whole other team that manages health and supplements policy. Each team has a set of guidelines they look to when evaluating whether or not to approve the banning of an ad or website.

If you are a repeat violator with no apparent signs of changing after being continually warned, they will take your case up to the Advertising Team to prosecute a suspension case. Unlike a court-room, where you can represent a defense of yourself before a judgment is rendered, you have no representation during this suspension process with Google. This process reminds me of the United States Foreign Intelligence Surveillance Act (FISA) secret court system, in that you don't know it is happening, you can't represent yourself, and you can't have representation to present a defense of you. Like FISA courts, which have an over-ninety-nine percent win rate for the prosecutors, the approval rate for requests from the policy team to the advertising team to suspend an account is very high.

How do you use this information about the Google Ads Policy team structure to your advantage? When you have an issue, focus on that specific team's mission and craft your responses or change your website in a way that speaks directly to that one team. Don't waste time trying to prove your innocence across the entire website. Instead, laser-target the specific policy they cite and their mission for that policy and show that you are compliant with each part of that policy through documentation.

A great example of how to do this is with a recent weight loss affiliate client I had. He had his ads disapproved for an "Insufficient Original Content" violation. This specific violation falls under the "Destination Experience" policy, and its mission reads: "We want consumers to have a good experience when they click on an ad, so ad destinations must offer unique value to users and be functional, useful, and easy to navigate." ("Google Policy Center", 2020)

This violation applied to my client because he didn't create a unique experience on his website. He had copied the parent company's website content onto his domain name, changed a few words to be slightly different from the other affiliates, and then ran his site on Google. If you look at the Google Ads Team mission for Destination Experience, my client's website would not be unique enough to qualify as compliant to Google.

To avoid a Destination Experience violation, I ask my clients these questions:

- Is there a compelling reason for visitors to buy from your site rather than to buy from the parent company website, instead?
- What additional value are you offering visitors that would make them want to purchase from you and pass up purchasing it directly from the parent company?

The answers to these two questions have helped my clients understand how unique their affiliate website needs to be from the parent company and other affiliates.

I had this particular client create a package of free courses visitors would receive if they purchased from them rather than if they bypassed them and purchased from the parent company. I had him do a Google Search for private label rights (PLR) content and had him buy labeling rights to content similar to his weight loss product to supplement it. PLR is a great way to add value to add value to your offer through an affiliate's website to distinguish your site from others.

Once my client had PLR content, I then redesigned his landing page around the bundled package of PLR and the parent company's product. These additions made his copywriting much more appealing than all the other affiliates'. Once he made the changes, I filled out a Google appeal form, documenting the mission statement's policy, the specific policy line under Insufficient Original Content, and the changes my client has made to meet this policy. His ads were approved forty-eight hours later.

I have a checklist that covers many of the Policy Team's checklist items they are looking for. I give it to all the clients I engage with, and we go through every aspect of it together. We then use it as a reference for items needed to be changed on my client's site, and to document every change they need to make. This one tip, of crafting specificity to the Google team's mission and the specific policy line—as well as referencing your changes directly to that team—will help you win a lot of your cases.

Download your free copy of the cheat sheet here:
www.compliancesecrets.com/cheatsheet

Google Ads Policy Center

Google Ads has a publicly available overview of the rules you must abide by as an advertiser. It is called The Google Ads Policy Center, and can be found by putting that name in a Google search.

If you are anything like I was back in 2009, I had never laid an eye on it or knew it existed. But you should take the time to review each area of concern and, most of all, pay attention to each team's mission in that section, as this will tell you the mindset of that policy team when confronting them. Don't make the same mistake I did. Familiarize yourself with the policy before it is too late, and doing so will save you a lot of heartburn and headache in the future.

That said, knowing the policy isn't a foolproof solution, as these individuals use subjectivity in decision making. This subjectivity is my biggest gripe with Google policy. Despite all of the subjectivity, based upon years of experience, getting policy decisions overturned is closely related to how well you meet the department's mission and how well you make the case your advertising is in line with their mission.

Google Ads Customer Support

Google Ads Customer Support is what Google calls the "reactive support," front line people you talk to on the phone or chat with online when you have an issue. They address the small stuff that is easy to fix without taking up policy resources. It is important to note: they have no power, but they get all the anger from advertisers. They, personally, did nothing wrong, but regardless they are the ones who get screamed at over the phone. I feel bad for them. That said, when you find a good one who has been around for a long time and can get things done for you, open up an email communication with them. Find out which location they work from (usually Mountainview, Ann Arbor, Boston, or New York) and ask for them whenever you can. A good reactive specialist can be worth their weight in gold. It is almost inevitable that you will end up triggering a Google bot at some point, and when that happens, you need a great advocate who knows how to reroute you to the right people to get things overturned.

The closer you can get to talking with a policy specialist or the editorial team, the better, as they specifically have the power to overturn policy issues. They can be tough to access, as there are internal rules about having as few people talk with them as possible. If you can't speak with one specifically, the next best thing an excellent reactive support person should do is mediate a chat session between you and them.

A Google compliance secret I learned from a sales rep years ago was to tell the reactive support person you talk to on the phone to put you "on hold" and "open up a chat ticket" live, right there, while you are on the phone. Have them chat with either the policy specialist or the editorial team responsible for your ad's violation and have them negotiate back and forth between you and them. Don't allow them to "get back to you" in twenty-four to forty-eight hours, unless you get a chat session opened up on your behalf first. This largely unknown insider tip has helped me through the years to get faster, more direct, and more accurate information to solve policy issues.

Now are you seeing why I took so much time explaining the Google policy team structure and the fact each team has their own policy mission? You will directly negotiate with them, and if you don't speak the language of "Google," you will lose. Your goal from this conversation with them is to either have the ban overturned (through you convincing them that you are within policy), or have such a good negotiation that they tell you precisely what is triggering the flag and how to fix it. You want to walk away from the conversation knowing the word, the page, or the phrasing in the ad that they have a problem with. This will only happen, though, if you have a two-sided conversation about policy and their mission, not just a one-sided rant about how you were wronged.

Summary

Google compliance is a combination of objective items and subjective items. If you want to make a Google-compliant website, it's important to know which departments are deciding what is compliant for your business model and the objective and subjective items they are looking for. The Advertising Team and the Google Policy Team work together to ensure a safe ecosystem for users—at the advertisers' expense, if need be. They are true believers in their mission. You must create your website with them in mind, as they are the ones who will derail your efforts to advertise. You need to understand what makes them tick. If you ever find yourself in trouble, identify if it's the Advertising Team or just the Google Policy Team that has a beef with you, read the specific team's mission statement, and then craft a response using their own words to overcome the problem. If your issue can't be resolved due to a legitimate violation, use this knowledge of how the company is structured to negotiate the specific changes needed, so you don't get vague answers.

Each Policy team has an internal "checklist" of objective and subjective things they are looking for to determine if a website is in compliance. In the next chapter, I will break down everything a website will need to run, including what information needs to be in each section of your website.

Before moving forward, I suggest you spend about thirty minutes going through the Google Ads Policy Center to familiarize yourself with each department's missions and start making your own compliance cheat sheet checklist just like I use with every client.

CHAPTER SIX

CHAPTER 7

Chapter 6

The "Core Four" to a Google-Compliant Website

If you skipped any chapter before this one, go back and read it, as what is coming in the next chapters will be hard to understand without the previous chapters' knowledge.

You now know who Google Ads is for and who it isn't for. This way, you won't make the mistake of trying Google Ads without the right business model. You have also learned how to avoid the mistakes other marketers make that get them banned before getting their first ads up and running. You have a good understanding of the Google Policy Team vs. the Advertising Team. You are finally ready to start building or restructuring your website to be Google compliant.

Building a Google-compliant website is relatively straightforward. Once you know the formula, you can make a template for each new vertical or website you enter into. Over the last eleven years, I have used this template for every client I have worked with, and my success rate for Google-approved websites is more than ninety percent. It isn't one hundred percent because, in all honesty, some marketers ignore what I say and do ill-advised marketing tactics.

Regardless of how many policy teams exist within Google, they all have a checklist. Over the years, I have compiled a list of things each department looks for when checking for compliance and have simplified it down to what I call the "Core Four." This represents the four main areas that make up a Google-compliant website:

1. Website Structure
2. Copywriting
3. Landing Page/Landing Page Funnel
4. Ads

The trick to winning the compliance game on Google is to give policy what they want (websites geared only to researchers and that feature substantial information) without losing what you want. Most marketers' goal is to target both buyers who are impulsive and buyers who are researchers. They use proven sales techniques, like minimizing landing page distractions that may reduce conversion rates. Having too much content or unnecessary links that add no value may make Google Policy happy with your website, but they do admittedly tend to reduce sales. The Core Four are designed to help you overcome this challenge and create a Win-Win-Win scenario—a win for you, a win for your buyer, and a win for Google.

An overview of each of the Core Four is described below.

Core #1: Website Structure

Website structure refers to your website design, its links, and any supplementing core business information. In a nutshell, it's your domain name and domain links. Most people think of this as the whole of a compliant website, but it is only one part.

Core #2: Copywriting

In this context, the definition of copywriting refers to the sales copy (headlines, body copy, and video content) of the website. I think of this as a separate part of the process from the website structure's content. Website structure content is designed to educate, while copywriting is intended to sell or persuade.

Core #3: Landing Page/Landing Page Funnels

For a direct response marketer, one-page websites can't be beaten—however, Google doesn't allow them. We have to give Google what they want while simultaneously getting the simplicity we want, in order to maximize sales. Number three of the Core Four has its own set of rules and set up, apart from the website structure rules and set up in Core #1.

Core #4: Ads

Core #4 doesn't seem like it belongs under website compliance, but your ad very much will determine the compliance of your website. The words or images you display, disclose, and use to sell in an ad will trigger policy to take action if your website structure doesn't align with what the ad promises. For this reason, ads are the first line of policing from Google for compliance.

Summary

There are four areas to Google Ads compliance, called the Core Four. These areas are 1. Website Structure, 2. Copywriting, 3. Landing Page and Landing Page Funnels, and 4. Ads. The Google policy team's checklist to judge your website and ads in terms of compliance will scrutinize your advertising in these four areas. You will need to know the parameters of each Core so you can apply the changes to your website. Let's start with Core #1 in the next chapter, and learn how to build the website structure.

CHAPTER SEVEN

Chapter 7

Core #1: Website Structure

Hub Content Site Structure

When building a website, you should always start with a firm foundation. Firm website foundations begin with the objective: the transparent business requirements of a website. This Hub Content is your website's first building blocks toward laying out the objective content of the website, in which all other content will be built upon.

What do I mean by "Hub Content?" Just like the traditional definition of a Hub, your website is the central location for the flow of all information. It is the place where all traffic and information go into, before being routed to the proper place.

Google's policy team's internal checklist consists of necessary items a website needs to have, and these items also must be easily navigated to and easily understood. How someone gets routed to that information when they land on your website will be crucial in lowering your overall risk score. Google will research your website and business information very closely, so you need to make it easy for them to do this. If they find it challenging to locate, navigate, and/or understand your website and business's essential details, they will be much more likely to take policy action against you. To make it easy for them to do their research, I created a Hub Content Site Structure.

The Hub Content Site Structure is designed to give the researchers and Google policy reviewers the bulk of what they need. Building the foundation of your website on this principle will give you more freedom to use more of the copy, funnel flow, and marketing strategies you want to use, with minimal raising of your risk score.

A huge foundational issue internet marketers often have with Google compliance is that they don't emphasize the top-level domain. Marketers typically don't want to send traffic there because sometimes there are too many distractions to click and info to consume, and that may hinder or slow sales. If you are anything like me, you would prefer to send all website visitors (traffic) to a landing page funnel to maximize sales rate. However, Google puts a great deal of emphasis on your Hub in determining your level of risk and adherence to policy. They still review landing pages and landing page funnels; however, they are much harsher on sites that lack the transparency and needed disclosures about the business, product, and how to navigate the website for information.

The Five-Second Rule

Google makes a lot of compliance decisions based on what I call the five-second rule. Within five seconds of landing on your Hub, they need to understand clearly who you are, what you do, and how you help people and/or businesses. This area of your website we often call "above the fold" because this area of the website is visible on your screen's browser window without having to scroll down. If you have to scroll down to see information, that additional information is considered "below the fold."

Many marketers unknowingly violate this internal rule because they want to drive curiosity with a headline, then push people to convert without any distractions. I am a huge fan of this process as it converts well. However, the job of the Hub Content is not to drive conversions, but to inform. Because the Hub delivers a more informational strategy, adhering to the five-second rule won't hurt conversions at all. Leave the emotional, suspense-filled marketing for the landing page funnel. For the Hub, you need to focus on delivering within the five-second rule. You can do this by first focusing on your website's hosting performance.

Page Load Time

The first Hub-centered item you need to focus on is page load time. Poor page load time is bad because the Google bots that scan your site are very quick, and if your website takes too long loading the different items on the page, the bot may deem the content, images, or even the whole page as non-functioning and disable your ads. It is essential to choose adequate hosting memory and speed for your website to keep up with Google's ad bots.

Website speed standards are updated and changed each year, so it's something you'll have to stay up-to-date on. When your website is finished, it is best to run your site through Google's PageSpeed Insights tool.

It is free to use: https://developers.google.com/speed/pagespeed/insights.

The tool will give you feedback about improvements you should make to your website to increase speed and reduce loading errors. They will break down desktop vs. mobile times as well. I suggest using the speed test tool at least once per year to ensure your site is keeping up with speed standards.

Video Load Time

Similar to page load speed is video load speed. With free video servers like YouTube and Vimeo, this is almost a moot point; however, this can become an issue for those who want to host their own videos. If you choose to host your own video, make sure you stay on the faster speeds when purchasing private servers. I am not a huge fan of hosting your own videos, as the cost becomes prohibitive. I recommend Vimeo Pro instead. They have a much better fee structure for small- and medium-sized businesses who want to host videos privately.

Navigation Links

Your Hub will be filled with navigation links. Visitors to your Hub will be able to click and scroll to all the relevant information they need about your business, products, and services, as well as the general terms of doing business with your company. Basically, these links will have more detailed information to cover the requirements of Who You Are, What You Do, and How You Help People.

Ease Of Navigation

Your Hub will need to be easy to navigate so users can find relevant information more easily. The Google bot needs to be able to easily scan your site and its relevant links, title pages, descriptions, content, number of links, contact info, etc., to whitelist your site Hub.

Do Not Follow .txt

Do not include robot.txt "do not follow" files on your Hub. "Robot.txt do not follow files" are files you code on your landing page or the entire site that tell bots not to crawl your website. It is your way of not permitting Google bots to read anything on your landing page or website. This .txt file is a popular file to have on a website, especially in membership areas for privacy. However, marketers tend to use them to prevent automated competitor spy tools from reading and caching (taking a picture of all the content, images, and videos on a website) their marketing material. They do this because, as a marketer, there is nothing worse than seeing your secret split test logged for anyone to see.

For this reason, marketers end up blocking all bots from viewing their website. However, the "do not follow" files add risk points to your website. In the Google Ads Terms and Conditions, there is a section that says if you block the Google bot from scanning any landing page of your site, Google will give your landing page or site a low-quality score since it can't read what's on the page. The bot may also decide you are deceptive by hiding critical landing page information and may slap your site with an Untrustworthy Promotions policy violation. I wouldn't have a "do not follow" file on your site unless it is on your secured, private pages. Checkout pages or membership areas where there are privacy concerns for the buyer are good examples of pages where you are not penalized for having a robot.txt "do not follow" file.

The lesson here is to allow access to all users, both bot and human, to your entire Hub, unless it is a user safety concern.

Hub Links

The next sections will cover exactly what navigation links are required on a Hub Content site structure and the information you will need to have within those pages. Some navigation links will be recommended to be placed at the top of the page because of the importance of transparency. Other navigation links will be fine to place in the footer, if you choose.

Homepage

Where are all of these Hub links and content connected? Answer: your homepage. This is the Grand Central Station of your Hub Content Site Structure, where every researcher can decide which train they will take to learn more about your business. Google prefers that you use a homepage as your central Hub location. Make your homepage the top-level domain name of your website. The alternatives (index page, about us, contact us), although they meet the five-second rule, would not provide the site's best user experience.

The way you structure your homepage is relatively straightforward. It is a small overview of every section of the Hub Content. From top to bottom, it will start with good load time, have a nice logo, follow the five-second rule, have top navigation, and include a "products" section, an "about us" section, a "how it works overview" section, footer navigation, a "contact us" section, a "services" section, a footer paragraph disclaimer (if required for your business), your business name, your business address, and your business phone number. Some marketers add blogs, articles, index page links, and other navigation types to their homepages. This is not required, but can add to the overall positive user experience of your website Hub.

Only an overview of each section is needed on the homepage, so you don't need to duplicate everything on the other pages—just have something to help the researcher understand what they will find on your Hub.

You also don't need to make the landing pages you plan to drive traffic to accessible from the homepage. Opt-in offers are allowed for lead generation or to start the process of a homepage funnel. Keep in mind, homepage offers are the most scrutinized by Google, since it's the top-level domain name, so make sure you don't push the envelope with your website copy. Keep the copywriting impactful, but no strong claims that will need substantiation (See Chapter 8 to learn more about claim substantiation).

About Us

Other than the Contact Us link, the About Us link is probably the most critical of your entire Hub. It is placed at the top of your page, as a general rule, for increased transparency. This page's role is to communicate in more detail the answers to questions like, "Who are you? "What do you do?" and "How do you serve people?" It can get into details of who is behind the company, the history, the industry or vertical focus, expertise, locations, expansions, etc. This page isn't about hard-hitting copy. It's about objectivity and transparency. This is a very traditional place for information, and you want to keep it that way.

What is most important to do here is divulge the details. Don't hide important information Google would want to know, such as who is behind the company, the industry you are in or whether you are a manufacturer or distributor. The more transparent you are, the more likely Google will accept it and not needlessly dig any further into your company.

Pricing

Price transparency is a cornerstone policy for Google. You will need a navigation link that indicates the details of your pricing. "Pricing," "Packages," "Products," "Training," or some other name that means the link will cover the cost of products will work. Oftentimes, marketers choose to put this information on the products page, which is also an acceptable location.

One exception to having a separate link with pricing information is supplement marketers who focus on the pricing right on the homepage. If you choose to disclose your pricing model on the homepage, having a separate link isn't necessary. In consultancy businesses, pricing can vary from customer to customer based upon the scope of work, so listing the price amount won't be as important as documenting the fact there is a service available with details about what the service covers. However, most of the marketers I have worked with through the years tend to have a very standard pricing structure that doesn't change unless they are offering discounts or package deals from time to time. Therefore, most people will have to list the prices of products on the website.

You are only required to list the regular, standard pricing, not any discounts or packages. On this pricing page, disclosing upsell costs are not required. Your main products or services are required. This leaves a lot of room to experiment with upsells for those of you who sell affiliate products or change your upsells frequently based upon the best ROI metrics.

FAQ

The FAQ navigation link can be either in the footer or header. This link is exactly what it sounds like: the most frequently asked questions about your business, products, or services. There is no minimum or maximum amount of questions you need to have. Instead, put yourself in your buyer's shoes and handle objections. Some common questions to put in an FAQ are, "What is (product name)?" "How does it work?" "What is your refund policy?" "How do I contact support?"

A word of caution for your copywriting here: if you sell any performance-improving products, such as supplements, diet or exercise products, finance, crypto, or the like, you mustn't promise anything. Instead, focus on what your other clients have reported and let the reader know that individual results vary. I will cover compliant copywriting in more detail in Chapter 8.

Products/Services Page

A central area to find all the information about your products and services will be needed. In this navigation link, which should be above the fold, outline what products (digital, selling leads, apps, training courses, or physical) and services (coaching, consulting, or labor-oriented) you provide in detail, and what your customer receives. Copywriting is allowed here, but more importantly, the details of each product, service, package, training, etc., should be outlined quite clearly.

If you choose to outsource your copywriting, make sure who you hire reads Chapter 8 first. Chapter 8 teaches the rules of compliant copywriting for Google Ads. Sales letters (article style pages), VSLs (video sales letters), Opt-Ins (forms that collect personal information to create a contact lead), and downloads (software downloads that are initiated by user request, usually by clicking a download button) are allowable on the product pages as long as the page's goal is to convert researchers. When writing copy for these pages, Hub content is reviewed the most by Google policy, more than your landing pages. Use less hype and hyperbole with your copy here. Elaborate more on the details of the products and don't use urgency techniques, such as countdown timers.

Pricing for each product should be disclosed if you don't have a separate pricing page, but retail pricing is all that is required. Having your retail price listed here may help your marketing when you claim the value of a product typically has a higher retail price, but you are giving them a discount. Your pricing in the Hub section can help justify any discounted value proposition you choose to offer on a landing page to increase conversions.

A special note for lead- generation marketers: I recommend that instead of a specific page or language about a product, you instead have navigation links describing the different services you are facilitating for the visitor. For example, if you sell mortgage leads, then you may have additional links for HELOCs, Refinance, Home Equity Loans, 30-Year Mortgages, 15-Year Mortgage, etc., and describe a little about what you are providing in those areas.

How It Works

How It Works is a navigation area of your Hub that explains how the process of working with you, your product, or your services work. Not every business will be required to have this link. Some business models have "how it works" inherent in their product description, which makes this information redundant (i.e., supplements, cell phones, or cars). That being said, if you sell consulting services, diet and exercise programs, lead generation, or similar products, you will need to disclose how your services work in a link. I suggest a paragraph overview with supporting images showing steps involved in your services or how to use your products. Traditionally, this link is at the top of the Hub or above the fold.

Contact Us

A Contact Us link is the most crucial link to have on a website. Although this is a very traditional link for a website, direct response marketers frown upon having one on their website or landing page. Regardless, Google considers your Contact Us area's information to be the chief cornerstone of your website's business transparency. If you fail to have the required information in this link, your risk score often escalates to higher levels.

Have this link at the top or in your Hub footer. My recommendation to have the link at the top. This is not a place for copywriting, but relatively objective information for business transparency. There are some special requirements for the contact page:

a. List the business name of who owns the website and the company advertising the site. A mistake here would be to only list the domain name as the business when another company owns, operates, and runs the website. Not disclosing the owning company is considered deceitful. If your LLC is the actual business that owns everything, sells the products, files the taxes, and ships the products, but on the website, you make it appear that you are doing business under another name or unofficial "doing business as" (DBA) company, make sure you list your LLC name in the contact section. For example, if you own Example LLC, and Example LLC is the company behind your website, but you do not disclose this information on the website (instead choosing to list the business name as the website address, www.example.com), Google may consider this website to be an Untrustworthy Promotion due to lack of transparency and disclosure of who owns this business. To fix this, simply add the LLC name. This will eliminate the violation.

b. Next, list the business operations address. Your business's physical location needs disclosed, not just the mailing address. Google owns Google Maps, and part of the background checks it runs on each website is to look up the location listed. If UPS, FedEx, USPS, or other mailbox addresses show up, you're in trouble. The reason you will be in trouble if you use a mailbox as your operational address is because Google knows you are not operating out of a mailbox. They own Google Maps. They will map your business location to see what is there. They will know you are not operating at that location. Google claims that by not having your actual operational address listed, this will give consumers limited options to contact you to resolve problems they may have with your product or your business. Google believes businesses who don't provide their operational address have a poor user experience for their searchers. Even worse than not providing your operational address and only a mailing address is you lying about the location of your operational address, and Google finds out. This will get you banned immediately from Google for Untrustworthy Promotions and Circumventing Systems policy violations.

This level of disclosure may give work-at-home marketers heartburn, because they don't want to let the whole world know their home address. There are a few ways around this dilemma:

1. Rent an office and list that address. I like Regus locations for this. It's cheap, and you can have real office space to use for legitimacy, to have meetings, to raise capital, or to do deals offline.
2. Ask your friend or neighbor if they would be willing to let you

run operations out of their home. This doesn't mean you actually have to go there, but their home would act similarly to a registered agent's office.

3. If you have physical products you ship, you can make your manufacturing location a "place of business" operation.

c. You also must have a designated phone line for your business. It doesn't matter if it is a virtual voicemail system or a hardline where you have someone answering the phone calls, as long as you have a dedicated line people can call, hear your business name, and leave messages.

Privacy Policy

It goes without saying in today's world of privacy, you are going to need a privacy policy link. Your privacy policy link is typically in the footer of your Hub. Google has five requirements they look for in a privacy policy:

1. What information do you collect?
2. What do you use that information for, and how do you store it?
3. Do you sell or share information with third parties?
4. Cookies and beacons disclosure, and
5. How do people opt out of you using or storing their information?

Lets dive into these five points.

1. What Information Do You Collect?

When disclosing what information you collect, you only need to disclose what you actually know you are collecting. For example, if you collect people's names, addresses, phone numbers, credit card numbers, and email addresses to process a payment or ship the product, you are only required to disclose that you are collecting those items. Other standard items listed are tax ID numbers, country, and gender. If you compile those, disclose that as well. Many of you will also have third-party tools (software tools you are using owned by another company) on your website to track visitors, and these may collect different pieces of information, too. You are not responsible for disclosing all the information they will collect. They are responsible for disclosing their collected information on their website.

2. What Will You Use That Information For, and How Do You Store It?

Explaining what you will do with the information you collect can be as straightforward as disclosing the steps required to process payments for a purchase. Common explanations used on most websites describe how your business uses the information to process purchase payments, deliver purchased products or purchased services, email receipts, send them special offers, give a quote, or sign up for a newsletter. Disclosing how you plan to store their personal information only pertains to sensitive portions of personal information, such as credit card details and tax ID numbers. The most common way to disclose how you store sensitive personal information is to talk about how data is secured and entered into forms on your website.

Here is an example paragraph you may model to meet the information storage disclosure requirement:

"Sensitive information, such as credit card numbers, is encrypted and protected as well as processed through a reputable, industry-standard payment processor. Our customers' information—not just the sensitive information mentioned above—is restricted in our offices. Only employees who need the information to perform a specific job (e.g., our billing clerk or a customer service representative) are granted access to the sensitive information."

3. Do You Sell or Share Personal Information With Third Parties?

If you do not sell personal information to third parties, simply add a line that says, "We will not sell or distribute your personal information to any third-party."

However, third-party lead aggregators (such as insurance lead generators who sell their leads to insurance brokers) and other businesses whose primary model is to sell the information to third parties must disclose that, by using your site and submitting personal data, the user is giving you the right to sell that information lawfully. Also, you need to disclose the reasons you may be selling that personal information and to whom (general categories only are required). This section of the privacy policy can "get into the weeds." Below is a typical example I have my clients use as a template:

"We also may collect personal and non-personal information in a form. We may collect, use, transfer, sell, and disclose such information for any legal purpose. For example, when you use our services, we may collect data from and about the "commercial electronic mail messages" and "transactional or relationship messages" (as such terms are defined in the CAN-SPAM Act (15 U.S.C. 7702 et. seq.)) that are sent to your email accounts. We collect such commercial transactional messages so we can better understand the behavior of the senders of such messages and our customer behavior so we can improve our products and such messages. However, if we do disclose such messages or data, all sensitive information contained in such messages will be removed prior to any such disclosure."

Check with the business buying the personal information to see if they would like you to add additional information to the above example and have a complete disclosure in this section.

4. Tracking Cookies and Beacons

This is where you lump all the necessary information about third-party tools you use on your website and how they track visitors. Although you are not required to disclose what information your third-party tools are tracking, you are required to disclose the fact you have third-party tracking on your site and how they work. Here is an example of how to write your tracking cookies and beacons privacy policy:

"Like many other commercial sites, our site utilizes standard technologies called "cookies" and clear GIFs to collect information about how our site is used.

"**Cookies:** A cookie is a small data text file which a website stores on your computer's hard drive (if your web browser permits) that can later be retrieved to identify you to us. Cookies were designed to help a website recognize a user's browser as a previous visitor and thus save and remember any preferences that may have been set while the user was browsing the site. A cookie cannot be read by a website other than the one that set the cookie. A cookie cannot pass on a computer virus or capture any personally identifiable information."

"**Clear GIFs:** At times, we work with third-party service partners that employ clear GIFs (also known as pixel tags, single-pixel GIFs, web beacons, or action tags) for our benefit to help us measure advertising effectiveness. Clear GIFs are tiny graphics with a unique identifier, similar in function to cookies, and are used to track the online movements of our users. The main difference between the two is that clear GIFs are invisible on the page and are much smaller, about the size of the period at the end of this sentence. Clear GIFs are not tied to your personally identifiable information and only track the visitor traffic and behavior to and on our site. Clear GIFs can "work with" existing cookies on a computer if they are both from the same website or advertising company. That means, for example, that if a person visited "www.companyX.com," which uses an advertising company's clear GIF, the website would match the clear GIF's identifier and the advertising company's cookie ID number to show the past online behavior for that computer. This collected information can be shared with the advertising company. We do, at times, provide such information to our third-party advertising service partners, but that information never includes personally identifiable information."

5. How do people opt out of you using or storing their information?

People have the right to disengage contact with you. Whether it be by email, phone call, or mail, users who have opted into contact from you need the ability to reach out to you and tell you to remove them from your contact list. When a client sends an email or calls you on the phone, accomplishing this should be relatively easy.

Have a link to unsubscribe from your list if it's an email, or if it's a phone call, process their request manually when you get off the phone. For those who use autoresponder services (broadcast email message services) like Constant Contact or Survey Monkey, opt-out links come standard in every email broadcast sent. However, if you are manually sending emails to people and not using an autoresponder service, this option won't be available.

For this reason, you will need to instruct in your privacy policy how people can proactively reach out to you and request they be unsubscribed from your list and have their information removed from your database. I suggest having a sentence in your privacy policy that addresses both scenarios. For example, I often use this as standard text:

"All newsletters sent to you from us include an "unsubscribe" link in them. You can remove yourself at any time from our newsletters by clicking on the unsubscribe link. Alternatively, you may also request to be unsubscribed or have your information removed from our database by emailing "support@example.com" from the email associated with your account and putting "Remove From List" in the subject line."

Also, Google requires you to adhere to local laws in your country, state, or municipality. They don't keep track of all the laws around the world, so it will be up to you to make sure you adhere on your own. For those advertising in the European Union and the UK, you will be responsible for making sure your company is General Data Protection Regulation (GDPR) compliant. GDPR is the EU's law on how websites should protect user data.

Terms and Conditions

The Terms and Conditions link, sometimes called the Terms page or Terms of Use, is a standardized page typically found in your Hub footer. It is somewhat legalized in nature and explains the terms of using the website, products, content, and other information on the website. It is a great place to house your subscription policy, refund policy, and additional necessary information concerning the conditions that apply to doing business with you. Make sure you consult your attorney about this page, as what you put here may open you up to legal liability.

Business Name and Address

Down in your Hub footer area, include your business name, business address, and, if possible, business phone number, although the phone number is optional. Keep the font size at a reasonable size, similar to the surrounding text, and don't "gray out" the text—it needs to be able to be read easily. I usually put this information in the same line as my reserved copyright information, in the footer area below my footer links.

Refund Policy

You must have a standardized refund policy, and it must be consistent across your website. The exception will be a special offers refund policy that only applies to the specific offer. Don't mix up refund policies across different pages of your site. This can lead to complaints about dishonesty when refunds are requested.

Once you have a policy, honor it.

You are not required to give refunds, but regardless if you do or not, you will need to have a clear refund policy. If you don't provide refunds, you will need a refund policy stating that all sales are final and no refunds will be given. This section of your Hub can be a stand-alone link in the footer, or you can add this section to your terms and conditions page.

There are five items required in every refund policy where refunds are issued:

1. What is your policy (do you provide refunds or not)?
2. Who is eligible to request one?
3. How to request a refund?
4. When will the refund be issued?
5. How will the refund be issued (i.e., back to the credit card of purchase or in a mailed check)?

Disclaimer

The disclaimer section of your website is going to come in two forms:

1. a disclaimer link all websites will have, and
2. a disclaimer paragraph for websites that make claims about results.

First, each website will have to have a disclaimer link, usually in the Hub footer. This disclaimer is for your protection. It is designed to disclose all the ways you aren't liable for what happens to the user of your site, its content, or your products. Those who sell financial, weight loss, or business success products definitely need to take heed when it comes to this section, to make sure it is thorough.

It is best to consult your attorney and competitor websites to see how they are handling their disclaimers for your specific industry. Creating this link may help to legally "cover your hiney" if you run across a litigious purchaser. Since I am not an attorney, I cannot give you legal advice about what to say in this section. For educational purposes only, here is an example of information one might consider placing in their disclaimer link if they are promoting a multi-level marketing business (MLM):

"Any earnings or income statements or examples are estimates for illustration purposes only. They are not to be considered standard or typical. There are no assurances you will do as well as the stated examples. Where specific results are used and attributed to an individual or business, those persons or businesses are anecdotal. There are no assurances you will do as well. Any and all claims or representations as to results in any form on this website are not to be considered as average results. Testimonials are not representative of the average experience of users of our products or website.

"There can be no assurance that any prior success or result can be used as an indication of your future success or results.

"Results are based on many factors, so therefore, we cannot guarantee or imply that you will achieve any results at all.

"Businesses such as this have unknown risks and are not suitable for everyone. Making decisions based on any information presented in our products, services, or website should be done only with the knowledge that you could experience significant losses or make no money at all.

"All products and services by our company are for educational and informational purposes only. Use caution and seek the advice of qualified professionals. Check with your accountant, lawyer, or professional advisor before acting on this or any information on our website or marketing material.

"Users of our product, services, and website are advised to do their due diligence when it comes to making business decisions. Your qualified professionals should independently verify all information, products, and services that have been provided. Our information, products, and services on this website should be carefully considered and evaluated before reaching a business decision on whether to rely on them. All disclosures and disclaimers made herein or on our site apply equally to any offers, prizes, or incentives that may be made by our company.

"You agree going forward that our company is not responsible for the success or failure of your business decisions relating to any information presented by our company, company products, or company services."

The second disclaimer, in the form of a paragraph in the footer of your Hub, is an additional requirement for sites that have specific claims of results, such as weight loss, supplement claims, financial claims, and claims of business success. This paragraph summarizes the disclaimer link and how the user should view the claims made throughout the Hub or website.

Here is an example of an MLM business opportunity's second disclaimer:

"*DISCLAIMER: Individual results vary. The sales and revenue figures stated above are my personal figures and are for illustration purposes only. My results are not typical. I am not implying you'll duplicate them (or do anything, for that matter). I have benefitted from practicing multi-level marketing and advertising for several years and have an established following as a result. The average person who starts a small business, even MLM, gets little to no results. Starting a business is difficult, and many don't follow through or implement what they learn. Your results will vary and depend on many factors, including but not limited to your background, experience, and work ethic. All business entails risk, as well as massive and consistent effort and action."

There may be additional legal requirements as well that need to be added to this paragraph. For example, supplement marketers are required to add the standard FDA disclaimer to all their footer disclaimers. In these disclaimers, make sure you cover the conditions that apply to any results claimed, like whether or not the results advertised are typical and what the typical results are, any applicable FDA or local laws, and the parameters in which the claims were achieved.

If that supplement marketer is promoting a weight loss aid, their footer disclaimer may read like this:

"The products and the claims made about specific products on or through this site have not been evaluated by the United States Food and Drug Administration and are not intended to diagnose, treat, cure or prevent disease. The information provided on this site is for informational and educational purposes only and is not intended as a substitute for advice from your physician or other health care professional, or any information contained on or in any product label or packaging. You should not use the information on this site for diagnosis or treatment of any health problem or for prescription of any medication or other treatment. You should consult with a healthcare professional before starting any diet, exercise, or supplementation program, before taking any medication, or if you have or suspect you might have a health problem."

Throughout your copy, you may have to make references to your disclaimer if you have a noteworthy claim. Do so by noting an asterisk at the end of the sentence that has the claim. This is a signal to users and Google that there is a further explanation of the claim in the footer.

We will discuss in more detail claims that need substantiation with a disclaimer notation in Chapter 8.

Website Design

Often overlooked is the actual design appeal of the website. I wouldn't call it a "requirement," per se, that your site is visually appealing; however, there should be a minimum standard applied to the appearance of your website, and every marketer should ask themselves this question: "Does my site look good?" I add this to my clients' requirements because of the subjective nature of the policy team. To them, Hub Content that "looks nice" is more legitimate and safer for the user. You don't need to go overboard with the design. Still, given the amount of information you will be divulging on your website, if you don't lay out your website in an appealing way, Google may think you are hiding information intentionally by making the readability low. So, get a good designer or template system that makes your site design look suitable for your Hub. Top the homepage off with a good site design and color scheme for user experience, and make sure the links from your Hub have an excellent design as well.

Summary

The Hub Content site structure is the foundation of your entire compliant website. Google policy will spend most of their evaluations going through your Hub Content. Engagement begins at the top-level domain name, which should be your homepage and overview for the entire Hub. Once you complete the Hub Content and create a good site design, you will be ready for the next step of the process: compliant copywriting.

FREE!

Google Compliance Cheat Sheet

Get Your Free Copy Of My Compliance Checklist...

FREE *Instant Download*

Enter your name and best email below to receive you a FREE copy of my "Google Compliance Cheat Sheet"

Download Your Copy!

...Use The Same Google Compliance Checklist Hundreds Of My Clients Use & Make Your Website Compliant in <u>Fraction Of the Time</u>!

Download your free copy of the cheat sheet here: www.compliancesecrets.com/cheatsheet

CHAPTER EIGHT

Chapter 8

Core #2: Compliant Copywriting

"I Made $9,480 In 1 Week Using This Simple, Foolproof, Completely Automated Online System from Home. You Can Too, Even If You Don't Know How To Email! Just "Carbon Copy" What I Do...I'll Teach You How!"

Ah yes...those were the marketing days. Back then, we would get away with hard-hitting, shocking, and overly hyperbolic copy that would entice even the most casual of viewers. Top the outrageous ad off by adding an image of me leaning on a Lamborghini sports car, and we have ourselves a real, lead-generating winner.

If you're laughing out loud right now, it may be because you have seen or maybe even written an ad like this, yourself. I'm ashamed to admit, I did too. It is no secret that Google does not allow such hyperbolic copywriting today. There are so many outrageous and unrealistic promises in the above copy, it's easy to see why Google Policy would have a problem with copywriting of that nature. Today, no one worth their salt writes misleading copy like the above on Google Ads—but nowadays, Google isn't even allowing marketers on with much milder copy.

Through lots of trial and error, I have learned how to write compelling copy that reliably gets the Google "thumbs up." In this chapter, you will learn the basic template for writing copy I use with every client to help their copywriters create the impact they want, while staying within the risk bounds of Google's rules. No matter your vertical or product, the following guidelines will help your copywriters frame every word they create.

That being said, compliant copywriting is a whole book in and of itself. Copywriters come in all shapes and sizes, and there are no two who have the same theory on what works best. However, with the following guidelines, you will at least be able to screen copywriters to see if they can adequately translate your message to the market in a Google-compliant and effective way.

To show you it is possible to adjust just about any copy into Google compliancy, I will use the ridiculous headline copy in the first sentence as an example throughout this chapter.

Claims

When we think of hard-hitting copy, we are talking about the claims we are making to the reader to get them excited about our solution to their problem. As a marketer, the claims about your product, service, or result are the juice that puts money in the bank.

Here is the good news for you: claims ARE allowed on Google Ads. Google has no problem with marketers making claims on their website.

The problem is that most marketers don't think about what claims they are making to the user. Marketers typically just copy the techniques marketing gurus make and don't think about the negative impact such claims may have on the people you make them to. I don't say that to make you feel guilty; I only say it because I did it too, and I want to raise your awareness of what you are doing so you can change.

It never occurred to me that only a tiny fraction of the people who read my promise to make them a millionaire could achieve it. Who knows, maybe no one will achieve it, even though I claimed it was as simple as "Carbon Copying" what I am doing. Perhaps my claim was technically possible, but by implying that result would be easier to achieve than it actually would have been, I was misleading the readers.

Google doesn't want your claims to be misleading, inaccurate, or unsubstantiated. Claims that aren't appropriate are often lies or deceit, whether intended as such or not. Often, you don't have the proof behind the claim from a credible source.

If you look at my previous copy, it violates each of those three: it was misleading, inaccurate, and unsubstantiated. Although I did honestly make $9,480 in one week, it is inaccurate that it was simple or foolproof. It was also misleading to say it was completely automated—-although I had automation in my system, it wasn't *completely* automated. Lastly, it was unsubstantiated to say that I could teach people how to do the same thing. I had no proven track record to show that anyone who learned from me duplicated the same results. Throwing money in people's faces as a claim, whether direct or implied, isn't allowed, as it cannot be substantiated that others could achieve the same, even if I did everything I could to help them.

Because of this, you have to do four things to a claim to make sure it isn't misleading, inaccurate, or unsubstantiated. You must Qualify, Quantify, Substantiate, and Disclose parameters and details of any claim you make that isn't considered widely accepted as truth, either by the public at large or deemed to be generally factual by known industry experts in the vertical you are in.

For example, if I claim that adults can lose one to two pounds per week through diet and exercise, I would not have to qualify, quantify, substantiate, or disclose the details of such a claim, because it is widely accepted by society and industry experts as fact. Although there are outliers to this claim, it is believed society's plurality would experience those results on average. For this reason, you can make similar claims without substantiation or source disclosures.

However, when your claims reach beyond what is widely accepted as truth, then you will need to qualify, quantify, substantiate, and disclose. There is an additional requirement for health and supplements: You can never claim to treat, diagnose, mitigate, or—more importantly—cure any disease. Marketing on disease or medical diagnoses-related topics are no-fly zones for marketers on Google Ads. Only FDA-regulated companies can advertise such products, and they are heavily regulated in what they can say.

How To Qualify Claims

As a general rule, claims can't run in the wild, meaning your claims can't apply to any and everyone in the world. Except for claims widely accepted as factual or patently true by the public, claims must be narrowly limited to precisely the persons who can achieve the desired result on average. To do this, put up guardrails in your copy and focus more on who is most likely to achieve the claims' desired result. In our example, I make a direct claim that anyone reading my copy can make $9,480 in a week if they use my system. It didn't matter if you were blind, deaf, a baby, or my ninety-four-year-old grandma who never even typed on a computer; I said anyone could do it. This is what I mean by a claim in the wild. It is running everywhere without any restraint, trying to entice anyone with a pulse.

To qualify my example, the first option is to pick out a subsection of people to whom the results wouldn't be a stretch. For example, I can narrow my audience down to focus on existing entrepreneurs who already run a seven-figure business. I can show them how to add $9,480 in a week to their top-line revenue. If did that, I would rewrite my copy to read something like this: "Attention Diamond Amway Business Owners: How I Added $9,480 to my Downline's Revenue in 1 Week by implementing This Online Lead Generation System Without Having To Dial For Dollars, Cold Call, or Use An Elevator Sales Pitch...Join My Webinar Today To Learn How Your Downline Can Use This System Too. I'll Teach You How!"

In this option, the qualifications are Diamond Amway business owners, revenue (instead of vaguely, "making money"), and I no longer said they could make the revenue numbers I did. At the time of this book's release, the average annual net operating income (NOI) of an Amway Diamond is just under $200,000, so adding $9,480 in a week isn't an unrealistic result a Diamond could achieve if given the right vehicle. However, I didn't promise I could help them do this. I only said they could implement the same system I did, and that I could teach them how. I didn't make a result promise. The claim is still considered implied, but since I am targeting an audience where the result is foreseeable, adding disclaimers on the page would be sufficient to keep the claim.

That being said, this copy would still have the desired effect on my target audience and convert rate. Yes, I would have fewer leads, but I would have a higher conversion rate with this audience because I narrowed my message to my exact target audience. Also, marketers who use copy like the original have over-inflated lead results anyway. This overinflation is evident, because every marketer I knew who made it big making promises like my initial noncompliant example is out of business today. They had to move on to another business or get a regular job because over time, most premium advertising networks banned the marketer from advertising on their network.

Another option—probably the best option—is not to entice people by claiming results at all, instead focusing on how the product or service can help them achieve *their* desired results. An easy example of this that still converts would be to change the above copy to this: "Entrepreneurs Wanted: Home Business Success Coach Looking to Train Rookie Internet Entrepreneurs on How He Makes Money Online. Free Course. Must Qualify. Only 10 Slots Available. Apply Today!" This example potentially would have similar results as the original example, but it's qualified much more and sets much better expectations. One could argue it may produce a better-quality lead, meaning it may be easier to close a sale.

How to Quantify Claims

Quantifying is all about the *numbers* in the parameters. By quantifying your claims, you add necessary realism and context.

I could very easily violate this rule: "Attention Diamond Amway Business Owners: How I Generate Endless Leads for my Downline Every Week…" By adding words like "endless" and "unlimited," I remove my claims' quantifications, making them misleading or inaccurate. Nothing in the world is unlimited. Everything has a finite number. Using phrases that quantify would be better, such as saying, "up to thirty leads a day."

In other verticals, such as weight loss or supplements, quantifying can take on the form of an age bracket, the degree of success, the time range of success, or whether the result is temporary only. For example, If you have a joint pain supplement, ask yourself if the claim about your supplement is running in the wild. Is it implied that taking the supplement will "permanently relieve ALL joint pain, no matter the reason you are experiencing the pain," or is it explicitly stated with a narrow reach, only claiming to specifically help "acute, exercise-induced joint pain?"

Here is another example applied to weight loss advertisers: an advertiser may be pushing an unquantified and unqualified weight loss claim that reads, "1 Trick to Lose 30 pounds of belly fat in 30 days." However, upon closer examination, the program details are directed toward helping menopausal women whose metabolisms are slowing due to naturally reducing estrogen levels. Their weight loss program is designed to aid the body's natural metabolism by adding more optimal timing to a menopausal women's eating pattern. Therefore, a reworked, quantified, and qualified claim may read, "Attention Women over 40: Lose *up to 30 pounds* by aiding your metabolism's optimal estrogen levels for weight loss by starting OMAD for Women."

One might think the first weight loss example is quantified and qualified because it mentions one trick, thirty pounds and thirty days; however, did it really quantify? Who, precisely, does this apply to? Does the trick work for everyone? What if I don't need to lose thirty pounds? Will I lose it anyway? Throwing in some specifics will add the clarity that kind of copy desperately needs.

Quantifying doesn't always have to be in text copy. Images are great communicators of quantification. I also recommend adding details in designated disclaimers and disclosures to give further details of the quantification.

How To Substantiate Claims

Substantiation is the "prove it" part of a claim. You have to have something to support your claim. It can't be wishful thinking, like in my original copy when I claimed I could teach anyone how to make $9,480 in one week. Case studies, medical studies, survey groups, clinical trials, tracked downline results, and pulling from publicly available information can be used as sources to add validity to your claims that what you have to offer can help people achieve the desired results.

A note to my "make money" marketers who promote "how to make money online"—don't just show pictures of your merchant account or affiliate back office, as if that is an adequate substantiation of a "make money" claim. I see so much of this right now on YouTube, and marketers think it is acceptable because Google hasn't kicked them off YouTube for doing it. The only reason they haven't been kicked off yet is because Google hasn't rolled out system-wide technology that can automatically detect these claims. YouTube still mostly manually reviews videos. They don't have enough policy reviewers to review the millions of videos being uploaded every day, but one day, the videos of marketers making such claims will be banned en masse.

Here is what Google requires from you: your site must realistically and accurately convey your product's benefits. Your site must be transparent to the user about any risks involved in using your product or service. To better comply with substantiation requirements, add original user reviews that are unique and credible (whole stories with proof sources are best), and add prominent disclaimers and notation references for more substantial claims that require more explanation.

For those of you who are marketing health and wellness products, especially supplement marketers, there is an additional layer if you are making structure/function claims under the substantiate requirement. Structure/Function claims describe the role of a nutrient or dietary ingredient's effect on the body's structure or function. Examples of common structure/function claims used by marketers are: "burns and blocks fat," "lowers blood pressure," or "breast enlargement supplement." These claims can be explicit (making a direct statement saying your product caused the structure/function changes) or implied, as in the case of using testimonial statements of your product users that claim they experienced a structure/function change while on your product.

Because structure/function claims are very close to drug-related claims, Google requires you to have something called "Substantial Substantiation." It is a mouthful, but this will be applied to all the claims you make for health and wellness, as well as for supplements with a structure/function claim. Substantial Substantiation refers to the need to cite credible third-party, unbiased sources for structural or functional claims as evidence of its truth or fact.

Suppose you claim your supplement helps relieve, remedy, or promote specific structure/function health improvements. In that case, you must reference a credible, unbiased, third-party source that has researched and validated your claims. Even if you did a study of your product for those claims, it still needs to be submitted to a credible, unbiased third-party to research and validate your results before you can use them.

And if that does happen, you have to use the claims very narrowly to what the group validated. For example, suppose you studied 1000mg of Vitamin C in men who are experiencing hair loss. You found that men between the ages of forty to fifty generally experienced a statistically significant improvement in hair growth when combined with a healthy diet. A credible third-party source, such as the American Medical Association, validated the results of the study. In that case, your claims in your copy must only refer to men between forty to fifty experiencing hair loss who take 1000mg of Vitamin C combined with a healthy diet. You cannot market your supplement with 1000mg of Vitamin C as a supplement that can stop hair loss for everyone, or even for all men.

I have found that very few supplement marketers overall have the funding, time, or resources to perform a credible supplement study for their product, which means they won't be able to claim their product affects the body's structure or function. Instead, I would recommend finding substantially substantiated studies performed for your ingredients list and cite their unbiased, credible sources. In this case, you can't claim your supplement has the desired effect, but you can claim that the ingredients to your supplement have been shown to deliver the desired effect and back it up with substantial substantiation (credible, unbiased sourcing) for each ingredient.

When it comes to ingredients substantiation, substantial substantiation only comes from one source: The National Institutes of Health (www.nih.gov). It is Google's number one trusted source for substantial substantiation of studies. Use reference notations that point to disclaimers at the bottom of the page in a superscript at the end of a sentence with a claim. This reference superscript number will help set up your disclosure of the substantiation.

How To Disclose Claims

Disclosure is listing out the parameters of the claim and citing sources for the claims. With weight loss products, for example, you need a paragraph that states the study group's size, how long the study was, the participants' average weight loss, and what percentage of the group achieved the promoted weight loss. You have seen disclosure statements many times. Weight loss commercials are full of asterisks at the end of a claim, which lead to a paragraph at the bottom of the screen with the study parameters. In the case of supplements, outlining research citations in the footer (similar to what you had to do in English class for research papers) is considered appropriate.

Note: since you cannot promote content relating to disease or medical diagnoses, you can't have such information in your citations either. For example, citing either www.examplecitiation.com/ diabetes or "Diabetes and supplements; JAMA 2020, published October 2020 issue" would not be allowed, as they reference a specific disease or disease treatments.

Don't Write Claim "Checks" That "Bounce" When Applied To The General User

Some of you will want to highlight the very best possible outcomes for your products. However, the stronger the promise or claim, the higher the risk score. Our goal is to keep your marketing strong and converting without raising your risk score above the unacceptable threshold. For that reason, don't write a copywriting claim "check" your product can't cash with the general audience.

Focusing on the best outcomes as an expected result will get you banned from Google. However, they do allow you to highlight one or two testimonials or case studies that show extraordinary results, as long as it isn't positioned as a norm. If you choose to take advantage of this, you will need to add a special disclaimer—and you can't highlight it above the fold, as above-the-fold items are considered core messaging. Here is the template I use for weight loss, but it can be altered for any vertical: "Results not typical. Average weight loss in the program over two weeks was "x" pounds. Individual results vary."

Urgency Sales Techniques

If you choose to use urgency sales techniques, like timers, countdowns, limited quantity, or specific dates the sale will last to get your reader to purchase the product quickly, it must be honest and trustworthy. Please don't add them as a marketing gimmick that you have no intention of following through on. I had one client whose ads kept getting disapproved for "misleading and inaccurate claims." Everything about the ad was Google Ads compliant. So I called Google to get in touch with a Google policy specialist to determine what my client was doing wrong. I found out from the policy specialist that he had a countdown timer on the landing page that stated a discount would disappear when the clock struck zero. However, if you refreshed the page, the clock would start back over, and the pricing remained at the discounted level. They told me to have the client either remove the timer and the urgency copywriting or follow through on making the users pay retail pricing once the clock struck zero. I asked my client why he had a timer he had no intention of honoring, and his response was, "because I was told it would increase sales." Urgency techniques that you don't intend to enforce are misleading to users and bad for Google's ecosystem.

Credibility Icons & Plugins

If you plan to use badges, third-party recommendations, "as seen on TV," "Proof" plugin technology, or other items designed to give your site credibility, make sure they are real, honest, verifiable (by clicking to the source link for the information), and updated if the situation changes. Don't use statements from celebrities that you have not received express permission from (in writing) to use. The same goes for using others' trademarks.

Disclaimers

Disclaimers in the footer of the website are becoming the norm for marketers. In more high-risk verticals, it's almost a guarantee you are going to need them. If a footer disclaimer is necessary for your offer, I encourage you to keep it as a static paragraph on every page of your website.

A couple of verticals are going to require unique language in their respective disclaimers. First, financial services or money related products will need the "FTC regulated" disclaimer added. These can be rather lengthy so consult your attorney on the formal language. If you are teaching about making money, you will need to add the risk involved, the average earnings a typical person in your program makes, and a disclaimer that makes it clear you are not giving advice. Also, in the footer, you would need to disclose where the financial claims came from in your copy and the parameters in which they were obtained. After testimonials that have results claims, add "individual results vary" at the end of the testimonial.

Suppose you are in the health, supplements, or weight loss vertical. Your disclaimer will need to state that you don't offer medical advice, clients should consult a licensed physician first, and that individual results vary. If you are a supplement website, you will need the FDA-required disclaimer in your footer. You will need to state that your supplement's claims are based upon user testimonials and known studies on the involved ingredients. These are the minimum requirements. Make sure you ask your attorney about other disclosures needed for your product or service.

Testimonials

When using testimonials as part of your copywriting, as mentioned in the previous section, it is vital to put the appropriate disclaimers below each testimonial. Not all testimonials require disclaimers. If it is about a person's experience working with you or your team, generally, no disclaimer is needed. However, if they start talking about results in any capacity, you will need "individual results vary" at the end of the testimonial. If it is an extraordinary success testimonial that's beyond typical results your customers can expect, you need to add "Results not typical. Individual results vary" to the end. As stated in the section above, if functional or structural claims are made in a testimonial, you will need even more: "results not typical. Average weight loss was "x" over "y" timeframe. Individual results vary."

Point of caution: Don't use outrageously good testimonials, even if they are real. A testimony from someone who lost one hundred pounds in three months is such an outlier that you will raise your risk score too high. Keep testimonials surrounding the normal range of experiences or slightly outside of normal, if it is an excellent testimonial. But don't use elite stories, as a general rule.

Also, don't use words that are disease state-related words as well. If the Google bot detects a disease state trigger word, it will treat your website as if you are promoting the treatment, cure, or mitigation of a disease. This claim will result in your ads' automatic disapproval and may lead to your website getting banned—or worse, your Google Ads account suspended. Examples of disease state trigger words are high blood pressure (which Google will interpret as hypertension), high blood sugar (diabetes), insulin (insulin shots), 180/120, or other blood pressure readings (hypertension), chronic (interpreted as referring to disease), testosterone (interpreted as the drug testosterone), degeneration (progressive disease), etc. The above is not an exhaustive list, but enough of an example of disease state trigger words to help you understand where the lines are. However, you can use substitute phrases such as "erratic blood pressure," "support healthy blood sugar levels," "beta cell hormones," etc.

Summary

Compliant copywriting is all about being honest, realistic, accurate, and transparent. If you have claims about your product, make sure you Qualify, Quantify, Substantiate, and Disclose. Core #2 can be the most challenging of all the "Core Four" because it is the most subjective. When screening copywriters to hire, give them a copy of this book and have them read this chapter. After reading it, provide them with a test copy to edit compliantly and see how they do. Only hire the ones who truly get it. If you plan to sell items with structural/functional claims, make sure you don't forget to substantially substantiate the claims and disclose the sources with citations and links. Beware of disease and medical claims that are medical diagnoses. They will get you in trouble with policy. In conclusion, hard-hitting copy and claims are allowed. Make sure they aren't misleading, inaccurate, unsubstantiated, or undisclosed.

CHAPTER NINE

Chapter 9

Core #3: How To Create Compliant Landing Pages

I have learned through the years that the best way to satisfy Google and not kill your conversion rates is to build your compliant website in two parts. First part is the Hub Content site structure we went over in Chapter 7, which will act as your site foundation. The second part is your landing page and your landing page funnel.

Attaching The Landing Pages

Attaching landing pages to your completed Hub that drive visitors through a simple, systematic sales process is the best route. It has been tested by marketers and approved by the Google Ads Policy Team. The strategy is to spin landing page funnels off your Hub that can only be accessed by a visitor if they know the direct link location, which will only be accessed if they click an ad you create in Google Ads. This way, you limit the amount of content that is hard hitting on your site to less than five percent of your site's content, thus drastically reducing your risk score with Google Ads.

This technique is how my clients and students are able to stay on Google, yet still crush conversions. My clients are leaving their competition in bewilderment about how they are able to stay up on Google with those hard-hitting offers. In general, you can be more aggressive with your copy, offers, and sales strategies when you only attach your landing page funnels to your Hub this way, but there are still a few rules of the road you need to adhere to.

Subdomains of Top-Level Domain

When I stay "attach" to the Hub, I am referring to using a sub-domain of your top level domain name, not another website—i.e., www.example.com/landingpage or www.landingpage.example. com, not www.AnotherWebsite.com. Google will be able to scan this landing page, but the scan will go through your entire Hub Content, as well. This reduces the risk of the copy and offers in this funnel, since the landing page's percent of content will be low.

The Five-Second Rule Still Applies

The five-second rule will apply to your landing page as well. As a result, you will need to add a clickable logo and navigation, as well as any relevant disclaimers to your landing page. One difference between your Hub Content site structure and the landing page is where the navigation has to be located. All navigation on a landing page funnel can be in the footer, and the only item above the fold required will be your logo. This will help keep the distractions from your offer to a minimum. In addition, I have found Google doesn't cry "foul" if I reduce the amount of footer navigation as well.

In the next sections, I will list out what items I have found Google wants as a minimum to approve the landing pages.

Headline

This is required to achieve the five-second rule. Typically, your main claim is in the headline. Although on a landing page Google will give you broad freedom to say what you want, there are a few things you need to keep in mind about your claims. First, they can't be misleading or unsubstantiated. Second, they have to be accurate, qualified, quantified, and disclosed (if necessary). Refer to Chapter 8 on compliant copywriting for more details on how to qualify, qualify, disclose, and substantiate claims.

Product/Offer

You need to clearly communicate the landing page's offer (the same offer you communicated in the ad they clicked on). Visuals are great here, along with bullet points, paragraphs, and other information that gives your visitor clear information to convert.

Google does not care if you choose an opt-in form, physical product, information product, webinar, or if you are simply selling the opportunity to get more information. Basically, all products and offers are welcome. What they do care about is the disclosure of necessary information, so people know what they are taking action on.

Here's what to disclose about your product or offer:

1. Price Disclosures: If you are trying to sell something that costs money as a direct response to your ad, make sure you disclose the cost either on the landing page or the very next page in the

funnel. It's okay to drop an opt-in before disclosing price, as long as you clearly communicate why you are requesting this information upfront and what you will do with that information.

2. Billing Disclosures: Just like in the Hub, you are required to clearly communicate the billing terms of the sale. Is it a one-time payment or multiple payments? Pay now or pay later? These are the types of disclosures Google is looking for.

3. Subscription Disclosures: If you are choosing to add a subscription model to your offer, make sure you follow the same opt-in, subscription terms agreement, and billing paragraph parameters we discussed in Chapter 7.

4. Opt-in/Lead Generation Rules: Google requires lead generation forms to include your privacy policy link near your submit button for your form. Also, they require you to outline what people are going to get in exchange for their information. Be honest here. If you offer a free book in exchange for their personal information, but you plan to put them on a drip list, make sure you disclose you are going to email them marketing material outside of just giving them the offer. You will usually have to get creative so you don't reduce your conversion rate. One technique I have my clients use states that when the visitor signs up for a newsletter, they get the free book. However you choose to do this, just make sure you are honest.

5. If you are making health, financial, or results-based claims concerning your product or offer, make sure you also qualify, quantify, substantiate, and disclose relevant parameters and citations. See Chapter 8 for more details about how to do this.

Footer Navigation

As I stated before, there is less navigation needed on the landing page than in the Hub. All navigation, other than a clickable logo to go to the Hub, can be put in a footer navigation element. Here are the links you need to bring over: About Us, Disclaimer, Privacy Policy, and Contact Us. In addition to navigation, Google requires your business name and business address in the footer as well.

Exit Popups

Exit popups are allowed, as long as they are not too intrusive or excessive. They also cannot disable functionality of the exit. If you want to give people one more offer *before* they click the exit or back button, that is okay, as long as you only do this once per visit, not multiple times. A popular strategy is to show pop ups when people are in the area of the back button or the exit. If you pop it up then, before the user clicks the exit, you are in compliance. If you pop it up after people click exit or the back button, it is considered intrusive and not allowed.

This rule does not apply to cart button exits, however. If someone is in a checkout cart and they click the back button or exit, you are allowed one pop up to make sure they clicked exit on purpose and to inform them they will lose their place in the cart if they exit. This is not a place to do additional copywriting to convince them how awesome your product is. Google allows it here because many people accidently hit "back" and lose their cart—but you can only make them aware of this one time, and never again after that.

Video Sales Letter (VSL) Rules

If you choose to use salesmanship in the form of video instead of text on a page as your content delivery, make sure you have some text copy on the page. You don't need to prematurely give up the secrets of the offer, but you do need some text so the Google bot can read what your page is about. I recommend having, at minimum, a text headline (not an image of a headline) and text about the offer.

Magic Cart Button Rules

Many marketers use a "magic cart button" that pops up on a timer in the video. This is allowable, but with one compliance tweak. If you choose to use a magic cart button, make sure you give people the opportunity to move forward in your funnel without having to wait for the pop up to come. Google considers it a bad user experience to force people to watch twenty minutes of a video before they know what your offer is and how to purchase. As a result, you will need to give them a way to move forward when they are ready, without having to wait.

Three ways to do this:

1. Add your pricing or products link to the footer or header,
2. Add a paragraph below the video explaining that those ready to move forward can "click here," with "click here" being a link to the next step, or
3. Add below the video, "If you would rather read, click here" with a link to a sales letter.

If you choose Option 3, there are a few sales letter rules.

Sales Letter Rules

You can write as many pages as you want in a sales letter, but make sure you have the minimum footer navigation and a paragraph disclaimer in the footer (if necessary for your business, based upon claims), as well as purchase conditions clearly stated prior to any "add to cart" button. Make sure you have reviewed Chapter 8 thoroughly before deciding to write a long sales letter.

Summary

Attaching a Landing Page funnel to your Hub in the form of a subdomain will allow you to drastically reduce your risk score, freeing you up to do more of the marketing offers, funnel flow, and copywriting you really want to do. By only driving traffic to the landing page, you avoid the low conversion rates traditional websites receive. Once you have a firm grasp of the copywriting rules mentioned in Chapter 8, build and attach your landing page.

In the next chapter, we will discuss how to add upsells to your landing page and what requirements Google wants, so you can be as profitable as possible.

CHAPTER TEN

Chapter 10

Upsells Funnel

At this point, you probably can see your victory on the horizon. You should be doing quite a bit of internal self-talk about how to create a Google-compliant website that converts with these changes in mind.

You are nearly ready to create ads. Now that you have a compliant Hub and a compliant Landing Page, let's finish up and learn how to make the rest of your funnel compliant, from your upsells to your checkout cart, so you can be just as profitable as you were before the "red bar of death."

Upsells are allowed on Google Ads, whether they are order bumps, low ticket, high ticket, opt-in offers, downsell, backsale, package, or offer walls. You are allowed to do one-page and one-click upsells, and you can have as many upsells as you want on one or multiple pages. Also, you have the option to offer upsells before cart checkout and after cart checkout. You can offer instant purchases by clicking on each upsell, too. However, there are items you need to adhere to to make sure you are staying within compliance:

Five-second rule

First, the five-second rule still applies. Although you will have limited information on an upsell, you still need to make sure people understand just what is happening and who you are, what you do, and how this page helps them. To accomplish this, have your logo/ tagline on each upsell page. You also will need your footer with all the links, disclaimers, and business info from the previous pages. Present your offer above the fold, clearly, without confusion.

Product or Offer

Since this will, more than likely, be a one-page upsell, you will need to have all the necessary pricing, terms, product details, and billing information all on one page. Purchasers must agree to being billed or agree to add to cart by taking action with a manual click. Do not automatically opt people into your upsells; they must choose them. Lastly, you must provide an opportunity for people to decline your offer, either by exiting out of the page or providing clear and conspicuous opt-out links or buttons near the opt-in button or link.

Exit Popups

Exit popups are not the best decision on upsell pages. Though they are allowable to show once, they may severely hurt user experience and you may start logging complaints, especially if you have an exit popup on your landing page, as well. However, if you are comfortable with the risk increase, they are allowed. As always, the copy must be written compliantly.

Subscription Upsell

If you plan to offer a subscription service, like many coaching and supplement business owners do, make sure you clearly communicate what the subscription actually is. Don't just state they can get a discount if they do a subscription. Lay out the details.

Also, you will need to put a subscription paragraph above an opt-in box (unchecked) that is required for people to check before they are able to process billing. The details of that paragraph are the same as described in Chapter 7: Product/Services Page.

Checkout Cart Compliance

Checkout cart compliance focuses more on how you pass personal and billing details along than it does on actual page compliance. However, I will draw your attention to a common error people make on the cart and checkout pages: testimonials and promises of success. Marketers never want to miss an opportunity to write sales copy to make sure abandonment is at its absolute lowest, and the cart or checkout page is no exception. But don't make the mistake of putting wild testimonials with massive success—or, in the case of health and supplements, testimonials about diseases being healed. It would be a shame to do everything else right with your website, only to slip up here.

Testimonials are allowed on a checkout process, but keep them tame and compliant—or, if you plan to put a few more success promises, make sure they apply to the masses that buy your product, not the select few. The layout of this page is more watered down and simplistic, as Google assumes people now trust you enough to purchase, so minimal navigation is needed. Just add the footer navigation on this page. The above logo and navigations aren't needed here.

Be clear if there is a payment frequency for your product. If continuity (subscription billing) is involved in your product or service, have billing disclosure paragraphs either on the product overview page or on the submit page for the payment. The billing of continuity is disclosed in a paragraph summarizing the billing with a subsequent link to the terms and conditions for full terms disclosure. If you put this in the cart check out, an "opt-in" box (empty check box) is required along with the paragraph and link. In the section describing the continuity, you will need to disclose, 1. When the next billing occurs, 2. How much it will be, 3. Frequency of the billing, and 4. How to cancel. Within your terms and conditions, have a separate section detailing the subscription agreement terms more thoroughly than this brief one- or two-line overview.

A few more notes on the Checkout Cart:

1. Proper Secure Sockets Layer (SSL) Certificate. Having a properly secured and encrypted checkout process, or SSL, is a must with Google Ads compliance. Make sure nothing in the coding of your secured pages is broken and everything is coded correctly and securely. Google will often disable ads to websites for this—and label the site as "malware," oddly enough. Since merchants require this as well, I usually only see issues here because the developer made a coding mistake. Coding mistakes are taken very seriously by Google Ads due to the nature of who Google is...a coding company. So check and double-check your developer's work on these pages. You can double check this by putting each individual page that is supposed to be secured with SSL into the address bar of a browser and loading your page. Once your page is loaded, your website address name should start with "https" instead of "http," and in many browsers just to the left of your "https" there should be a "closed lock" icon.

If you instead see a "closed lock" with a red line through it, a letter "i" with a circle around it, no lock at all, or a scary warning about the site not being properly secure and a warning that the site may contain malware, then your SSL Certificate wasn't properly installed on your website and needs immediate correction by your developer or site coder. If you are hosting your site with a template website company such as Wix or Clickfunnels, contact support for that company and ask for "SSL help."

2. Don't pass along personal details in the web address bar. You will have an instant User Safety violation if you pass personal details, uncoded, through the address bar during the upsell or checkout process. Make sure personally identifiable information is coded so no one can hack, see, or store personal identifiable information without permission. If Google's bot detects any personal information being passed along by you in the address bar, you will get a nasty letter from Google saying you only have a few days to correct it before they shut your account down. Again, this is a developer issue. Make sure your developers are aware of the consequences of taking coding shortcuts that cause this issue.

3. Prices must match the offer. It is a violation of Google's Misrepresentation Policy to have misleading or inaccurate claims. If you offer one price on the sales page to get people to convert, you cannot change the price in the cart or checkout. You can easily make this mistake when split-testing (conducting performance improvement tests, comparing something new in marketing against existing marketing to see if the new can perform better) price points, as you might forget to make it all match up. Put this on a bullet point checklist of things your team needs to change when there is an A/B pricing test or pricing changes occurring.

Summary

Upsells are allowable. When you add your upsells to your landing page funnels, make sure you create a template that has all relevant information on each page so you don't forget anything. Common mistakes surround not disclosing all the terms, pricing, and billing information to get the sale, since marketers like to keep these one-page upsells skinny on copy to reduce distractions and make conversions easy. You can keep pages tight and skinny, but make sure you have proper disclosures. Lastly, you have developer liability here, with compliance. Make sure your developer clearly understands the importance of SSL security and information privacy of purchasers.

Once this part of your website is done, you are finally ready to upload or create your Google Ads account! All you need to do now is the last part of Google Ads compliance for your website, and that is to create Google-compliant ads.

CHAPTER ELEVEN

Chapter 11

Core #4: How To Write Compliant Ads

You are ready. Your landing page is ready, your Hub Content site structure is ready. All that is left to do is to create your first ad to drive traffic to your funnel.

A compliant ad is the last of the "Core Four" Google Policy will look at to determine if your website will be allowed to run. In this next section, we will discuss what makes up a Google-Compliant ad, what Google Policy will be specifically looking for, and how you need to structure your text and banner ads so they get fast approval. Once you get that down, you are off to the races to make money on Google Ads, which will give you a huge advantage over your competition who can't keep an ad up and running on Google.

What Google Looks for When Evaluating Ads

The largest vulnerability for Google is their ad network. Since ad impressions are very widespread and can communicate messages to the masses, Google considers it the largest risk score for them. A scam advertiser may get one thousand clicks in a single day and expose users to potentially harmful content on a website; however, before the advertiser even gets the one thousand clicks, they have exposed millions of people to an ad that may be misleading and hurt confidence in Google's ability to deliver relevant results for searchers. To deal with this before it becomes a problem for Google, their policy team and bots scan ads for compliance to ensure the safety of the viewer or site visitor. Let's go through what Google will be looking for.

Logo, Product, Website Name

The very first thing the Google bot and manual reviewer will look for when you create your first ad—and any ad for that matter—will be the proper transparency they need for User Safety. No matter your business model, Google wants users to be able to do a five-second rule on your ad. You don't need to disclose everything, but you do need to disclose enough so people can make an informed decision on whether or not to trust your ad enough to click it. Regardless of if you create a text ad or an image ad, Google will look for the following basic items first:

1. Your product or service,
2. Your logo or business name, and
3. your website (not your tracking link) in the ad.

For text ads, Google's ad creator tool forces you to put your website address into the ad. You have to manually place that information into your banner ads. For image ads, these three items must be legible. Don't make these items too small to read, or "grayed out." You can make these items a part of your copywriting if you like, but regardless, within five seconds they want people to be able to get a quick reading on your company from your disclosure of these three items.

Relate Ad Copy or Images to your Product or Service.

Your ad must relate to your product or service. You can't choose some random, unrelated headline, description, or image that does not relate to the services you provide. I see this violated often by advertisers who try to take their Native advertorial strategy to the Google Ads Display Network. In Native ads, it is very common to have a fake blog or article site in which the intent is to have people believe the content is just an extension of the website they were on, but in reality, they will bait and switch the readers into their product one or two clicks away from the landing page. Oftentimes the landing page experience is completely different from the business model of the seller using advertorials.

Clickbait is Banned.

Headlines, descriptions, and images whose only job is to draw attention without relating to your company or product are not allowed. This is called "clickbait," and it is banned on Google. Marketers use shocking images, such as guns pointing at the viewer, gross-looking food in the palm of a hand, a suggestive yellow banana with two apples below it, or images of overweight or overly skinny people in an effort to increase click-through-rate and break through the noise of the internet. However, such shocking or unrelated-to-product clickbait ads are no longer allowed on Google.

Follow Through on the Ad's Promise in One to Two Pages

Google will check if you are following through on your offer within one to two pages of the ad—and it must match up with the ad's offer. Don't make people jump through numerous prequalifying hoops before they can get to what you promised in your ad. Lead generators need to be very careful with this policy. Often lead generators make a promise in the ad, people land on their landing page, they are pre-sold an idea and click an affirmative button, then they are taken to a page that says they need to opt-in before even seeing what you have available. Only after opt-in can they see the real sales page and, after that, they can go to another page to purchase.

This is too many pages between the ad's promise and where people can get the promise. Don't overly prequalify clicks.

Don't Make Misleading or Inaccurate Claims.

Strong claims are allowed in ads; however, misleading claims and inaccurate claims are not. Key phrases like "Up to," "as little as," and "diet *plan*" can make misleading claims realistic claims, because you are making statements that will apply to the typical person who uses your product. See Chapter 8 for more thorough information on making proper claims that qualify, quantify, substantiate, and disclose in a way Google will approve.

Link your Ad's Destination URL to your Landing Page, not to a Tracking Tool.

Tracking conversions, demographics, and traffic is vital to a marketer's success. Every day, new and innovative tracking tools are created that allow marketers to know just about everything a visitor does on their website. If your tracking tool requires visitors to visit your website first before redirecting to your landing page, make sure you add the tracking URL in the extra parameter section of your ad, not as your final destination URL. If you use your tracking URL as your final destination URL, you run the risk of getting your account suspended if the company that created the tool gets suspended from Google or they don't properly code the tool to Google's standards. If you add the tracking URL in the designated tracking section in Google's ad creator tool, Google won't hold you responsible if there is a problem with the company or their tool. They will simply disapprove your ad and tell you to remove the third-party tool. Once you do that, your ads will run again.

Summary

Core #4, the highest potential risk-score core, is your ad. Google Policy will be keen on making sure your ad is directly correlated to your landing page. Make sure any ad you plan to create can deliver your ad's promise in one or two pages of the click. If not, you will need to restructure either your ad or the landing page funnel to accomplish this. Don't use clickbait to increase click-through-rate (the percentage of people who see your and choose to click it), or your ad will get banned.

Before you upload those first ads, ask yourself these four very important questions first: "Does my landing page not match my ad?" "Is the ad mainly 'clickbait?'" "Am I making any misleading or inaccurate claims in my ad?" and lastly, "Do I have my ad's final destination URL pointing to a third-party tracking page?" If the answer to any of those questions is "yes," make the necessary corrections first before you save your ads in Google's ad system to avoid Google raising the risk score of your account.

CHAPTER TWELVE

Chapter 12

Google Ads Traffic Secret

Many marketers believe that the amount of traffic you are able to access on Google Ads is a function of keywords or placements and how much you are willing to spend to get that traffic on those keywords or placements. Although this is true in part, these aren't the major points in determining how much traffic Google will allow you to have.

I had a client named James who was promoting a supplement to help people suffering from joint pain get all-natural relief. James came to me for compliance help because Google had disapproved every ad in his account for a Misleading Claims violation. Any new ad he created, even if it was a "vanilla" ad (ads that only mention the product name and a button to buy the product) were getting disapproved for a Misleading Claims policy violation.

After researching his ads and his website, it was clear to me that his website wasn't compliant because he didn't have a Hub content site structure, his landing page funnel was full of unsubstantiated claims, and he didn't qualify, quantify, or disclose any claim on his entire website. To make matters worse, his keywords on Google Search had an overall average score of four out of ten, which is a below average quality score rating given to advertisers who Google doesn't think is very relevant to a keyword they are targeting or has a questionable ad or questionable website quality. In addition, upon evaluating his Google Display Network campaigns, I noticed his ad spend had been consistently declining each month over the last three months, and fell to the point where he was only able to spend approximately ten thousand dollars on ads in a month. Historically, he was able to spend fifty to sixty thousand in ad spend per month on average.

He was panicking and very emotional, barely holding it together. He told me he was two months away from closing his business if he doesn't get his ads back up and running, because he has to pay his American Express bill when it comes and he won't have the money to pay the bill and pay employee payroll because sales have been declining for months.

He kept saying, "Dathen, I need your help, now!" over and over again. "Please, please help me. I don't know what to do."

I had so much empathy for him. This wasn't the first time I had heard this level of desperation and fear of loss from someone trying to hire me. Every time I hear it, it reminds me why I'm so passionate about Google compliance—getting it right can literally be life-saving for my clients, their families, and their employees.

He hired me on the spot and we immediately went to work that day to make the proper changes. Within just a couple weeks, he had completely transformed his marketing to be Google-compliant. We deleted the old, noncompliant ads and uploaded the new, compliant ads to go to a compliant landing page and website. We also reached out to the Google Policy Team to make them aware of the changes we made so they could remove the penalties on my client's account. Within twenty-four hours, they had lifted the sanctions and his traffic started back up again.

He was so excited. He couldn't thank me enough for my help. I could almost feel the stress leave his body as we talked over the phone about the success he just had. "Thank you," he said, "You don't know how much you have saved me by helping me get this overturned. Thank you." I felt a great sense of joy for being able to help another client overcome the compliance huddle.

A few days later, though, I received an unscheduled phone call and I noticed it was James's number. I answered with a big smile on my face, assuming he was calling me to praise me some more. However, before I could even finish my greeting, he interrupted me, talking loudly, in another panic. I remember thinking, "Oh no. His ads are down again!"

He said in a loud voice, "Dathen, Google is spending ridiculous amounts of money and I can't stop it!"

He began to tell me that once his ads started back up again and he was getting traffic, everything went back to normal, at least for the first two days. However, on the third day, he woke up to his account having spent four times its normal daily spend. Normal spend for his account was two thousand dollars a day. By the time he checked his account that day, he had already spent eight thousand dollars.

You are probably wondering how it was possible Google would spend more than his daily budget. He had always set a higher daily campaign budget than what Google would actually allow him to spend. At the time, he had set his daily spending budget for his campaigns at four thousand per day, but at most, Google had only ever allowed him to spend two thousand in a single day. However, the third day after his newly compliant ads and compliant website was running, a new milestone was hit in only twelve hours of running ads. Before he knew it, James's campaigns had spent eight thousand dollars—and it was only 9am! He said he immediately paused all his campaigns in a rushed panic and started trying to figure out what happened. He also said that American Express had frozen his credit card, because Google had tried to bill him several times in a row in the morning and it triggered a fraud alert. His ad spend outpaced his sales, as sales of his product can take up to seven days to complete (because many of his clients needed a few days of cultivating on an email marketing list before actually making a purchase).

In short, money was flying out the door at an incredible pace. He was in hot water. He didn't have the money to pay Google, since he just started his ads back up and now his credit card was frozen for fraud alert. He was now having the exact opposite problem as he had in the beginning, but his business was experiencing the same threat of going under!

Even though he manually paused his ads, Google couldn't pause all of his ads fast enough due to the high volume of clicks he was getting across thousands of websites and keywords. He ended up spending an additional two thousand that day, *after* he paused his campaigns. By noon, Google had finally stopped all his ads from showing. When it was all said and done, he had spent ten thousand dollars over the morning hours. I felt so bad for him, but I was grateful I was having the opportunity to see something remarkable first hand. That day, I got a good glimpse at how much a noncompliant site and ads can hold back the success of a marketer, and just how important it is to do things right from the very beginning with compliance. I also teach the lessons learned from James's experience to my consulting clients. Teach them not only the Google Ads traffic secret of having a compliant website, but also the importance of lowering your campaign budget substantially before turning your ads live once you make your website Google compliant. The traffic may be too explosive to handle if your traffic had been limited by having a noncompliant website.

Although James's business was threatened to close down again, James actually went on to have his best month yet at that time. It took him about a day and a half to see that this new traffic was better than the old and people were more likely to purchase. Once he saw this, he calmed down, turned his campaigns back on, and was able to experience something truly amazing in his business that month. After turning his traffic back on (and lowering his campaign budget drastically) he learned this new premium traffic was much more responsive in every way to his compliant website. His conversion rate was 30% higher than normal. The average cart value grew by 53%. His chargeback rate fell from 1.9% down to 0.3% that month. The average time to purchase from people on his email list fell by 2 days. He called American Express and requested they lift the fraud alert for Google on his account, applied for a line of credit increase using his new sales numbers as support documentation for the request, which they approved. His company was the healthiest it had ever been, even though his company just a few weeks earlier was in jeopardy of going under. James went on to sell that supplement company for an eight figure evaluation and decided to retire from business building and is now a full-time investor.

In general, noncompliant marketers have misconceptions about how traffic is issued by Google, which may lead many of them to make poor decisions to push noncompliant content onto Google Ads. They believe they can "buy" their way into the most effective traffic on the network by paying more for a click on their ad or inputting a large ad spend budget into their network interface. If they had a good understanding of how Google awards traffic, they would realize they have only held their business back. Google only releases a tiny fraction of the traffic to accounts that have a low quality score and low ad rank.

Quality Score

So, just what are quality scores and ad ranks? Let's break down quality scores first. Your "quality score" is the measure of how useful, how safe, and how relevant your advertising is to the keywords and websites you choose to target with your ads.

On Google Search Network, you are able to see a visual representation of what your quality score is, on a scale of one to ten, with one being the lowest category of score. I call them categories because even within a level, there are different numbers assigned to desktop ads, mobile ads, tablet ads, and TV ads—however, the only visual representation you will see on Google Search Network is an average score of all these together.

You will be able to view your quality scores at the keyword level, as each keyword will have its own average quality score assigned. The higher the score, the higher relevance, higher usefulness, higher safety, and higher quality Google considers your advertising to be. They reward your efforts with more traffic, cheaper clicks, and a higher ad rank. In effect, you will get more traffic from your targeted keywords and websites, have your ads positioned higher up on Google Search, have better ad spots on websites, and it will be less expensive for you to advertise than your competitors who have poorer scores on those same targets.

Google Display Network also has quality scores assigned to your targeting, but they do them differently than the search side. They assign them by category of websites you are targeting as a whole, not to individual websites. They don't disclose any of your Display Network quality scores to the public, but they will give *you* a representation of your ad rank, which includes quality score as part of its equation (which we will discuss a little later).

There are several factors that make up your quality score: expected ad click-through-rate (percent of people who see your ad and click it), ad relevance to the keyword or website (how relevant and safe your ad is to the keyword or website your ad is shown on), ad compliance, and landing page relevance, quality, and compliance (the value of the landing page and website to solve the problem the visitor has).

Approximately forty to sixty percent of your quality score depends on the expected click-through-rate of an ad. This is because Google wants advertisers to create ads that get people's attention and compels them to click on it. However, once an advertiser realizes this fact, they may feel incentivized to create "clickbait" ads. As we discussed in Chapter 11, clickbait ads are against Google Ads policy—so to discourage them, Google weights approximately twenty to thirty-five percent of your quality score to ad relevance.

Ad relevance refers to the keywords and language you use for your ads, both text and images. The more closely associated your words and images are to the user's need, the higher your ad relevance scores will be. For example, if you did a Google search for the keyword "flat screen TVs," the ads that had the phrase "flat screen TVs" prominent in their ad will be given the higher relevance scores, but the ads that only mention "TVs" or "flat TV," although they are relevant, are not the *most* relevant ads to the user's question.

In addition, there are other keywords people who type in "flat screen TVs" often search in conjunction with their initial search. If you combine those keywords in addition to the most relevant keyword, your ad relevance scores will go even higher. Using the example above, you can infer that people would often add in the keyword "large." You can increase your ad relevance scores by having "flat screen TVs" prominently as the main headline, then adding the phrase, "large flat screen TVs" in the second headline or in the description headlines.

You can easily find these secondary keywords as suggestions in the Google Search bar when you start typing in the main keyword, or at the bottom of the Google Search results page near the footer.

Ad relevance has a compliance component to it, as well. Google wants your ads to speak to the needs of the searcher safely. What I mean by "safely" is that you are required to use language in the ad that would not lead the Google bot or the user to believe you are potentially promoting misleading or harmful content. When you are a noncompliant advertiser, your quality score suffers because you will routinely be assigned the lower quality score numbers. Also, when you have noncompliant content in your ads, the Google system may take additional punitive actions to encourage you to change your ads and make them compliant.

In order from least severe to most severe, the punitive actions Google may take are: lower quality scores (less than five out of ten), low impression share (meaning you get a lower percentage of available traffic), low ad rank (this will allow your competitors to get a higher position on the page than yours, because Google will choose to show their ad in the better positions that receive more of the clicks), impression caps (the Google system will restrict how much traffic your account is able to receive. Typically, you will only receive ten percent or less of available traffic), ad disapproval, site suspension, or account suspension. Many marketers believe that the only compliance recourse for ads is an ad disapproval or account suspension, but they fail to see the other actions Google is taking before deploying these two larger punitive actions.

Landing page relevance, quality, and compliance is the last factor in determining how much traffic an advertiser is eligible for, outside of your bid and budget. Landing page relevance speaks directly to the subject matter of the landing page and website, as it relates to the keywords the searcher typed in or the website they were on before they clicked your ad. How relevant is your landing page solution to fixing the immediate problem they were researching? A part of your quality score is how well Google thinks you did answering that question. You are encouraged to add keywords the user is looking for into your landing page to let the searcher know that you are relevant.

Also, landing page quality is taken into consideration. Did you follow through on your ad's promise? Is it easy to find relevant information on your landing page or website? Do people immediately leave your page within seconds and search again for another website that does a better job of meeting their needs? Is your website easy to use or understand? How well-coded is your site (meaning, is it easy for the bots to read, and does it load quickly and fully without errors)?

Your landing page and website's compliance will play a role in your quality scores, as well as ad rank. This is a two-sided evaluation. First, the Google bots will evaluate the landing page and website for compliance and give you assigned scores and ad rank accordingly. Second, the publishers (see Chapter 5) will assess your compliance when your ads show up on their websites, and if they see a potential violation, they will report your ads to Google to restrict your ads on their website. If you continue to get feedback from publishers to restrict your ads on their website due to compliance, Google may assign you a low quality score on the category of websites those publishers fall under. Your traffic will subsequently either cease running in that category or be drastically reduced.

In addition, the Google bots are scanning your landing pages and website for compliance violations or items that may be misleading or unsafe. If the bot finds noncompliant content it deems risky to users, it may start restricting your traffic volume or stop your ads from serving altogether.

Getting a lower quality score due to lack of compliance is only half the problem. The other issue noncompliance causes is a low ad rank.

Ad Rank

Ad rank is a measure of how likely your advertising is to beat out your competition and provide a good experience for people who click on your ads and visit your site. Your ad rank score will determine if your ad will be eligible to show on a keyword or website, what position on the page your ad will show compared to the ads of your competitors, how much more or less you will pay for a click than your competition, and the quality of websites you will be eligible to show ads on. For example, an ad on Google Search Network with the highest ad rank may show up on the left at the very top spot for ads, whereas the eighth-ranked ad may show up on the left side at the very bottom of the search results, right before you click to go on to the next page of Google's search results.

The calculation to determine your ad rank is rather convoluted and intentionally vague: Quality Score x (multiplied by) Bid (your cost per click "bid") x Ad Impact (which ad format are you using) = Your Ad Rank. Ad impact, in this equation basically refers to how much of Google's ad technology you are using in your ad. The more of Google's technology you use in your ad, such as using sitelink extensions (extra headline links), responsive ads (Google proprietary ad serving optimization tool), and HTML5 (banner ads that move), the higher your Ad Rank score will go.

Although this information is nice to know, what is most important is how much noncompliant advertising affects your Ad Rank. The first way it impacts you is with a low quality score. In a nutshell, when you have a low quality score, you have to be willing to pay considerably more money to get your ad shown on a keyword or in a page. For example, if you want your ad to show on your own product's keyword, but your quality score is low (below a five out of ten), then your competitors can more easily steal your potential customers away by advertising on your product's keywords and showing up higher on the search results at the top, above where your ads are showing.

Using the equation, let's see how this would play out: let's say your quality score is two out of ten on your own company's product keyword, due to poor Google compliance. You are willing to pay two dollars per click on your ad. If we ignore ad impact for this example, your potential ad rank for your product keyword is 4 (2 (quality score) x $2 (bid)). If your competitor has a quality score of five out of ten but is only willing to pay $0.81 for a click on your product keyword, assuming both of your ad impacts are the same, they will have an ad rank of 4.05, which is higher than your ad rank of 4. This means they will be positioned above your ad on your own keyword, potentially stealing a healthy amount of your customers.

On top of that, in this scenario, you will be paying considerably more for clicks than your competition. Your competitors are only paying $0.81 per click, while you have to pay two dollars per click. This means you will have to continue to pay drastically more per click than your competition if you want to keep your advertising above their ads. Also, if your competition decides to raise what they are willing to pay for a click on their ad to just one dollar instead of $0.81, then you would be forced to increase what you are willing to pay per click from two dollars up to $2.50, just to equal the same ad rank as your competitors. That is a twenty-five percent increase in cost, just to keep your own customer!

Summary

These two factors, quality score and ad rank, will tell the Google bot just how much traffic you are eligible to receive, regardless if you are targeting Google Search Network or Google Display Network. These equations are important for advertisers to know to help them understand how important being Google compliant is to the quality and quantity of the traffic you will be eligible to receive.

This is the hidden secret to traffic on Google Ads. Few advertisers know or understand it. Part of my services to clients who hire me for Google compliance assistance is to help them understand the avalanche of new traffic they may experience from having a fully compliant site. Many times, like with James, they struggle handing the volume of clicks and new potential customers sent to their website. They are getting visitors from new, premium websites (publicly known websites that are trusted and have a higher concentration of buying visitors) they weren't receiving before, and they are getting even more traffic from the keywords and websites they previously were advertising on.

Google reserves the highest levels of ad impressions, site visitors, cheaper clicks, and the best ad positions for their least risky advertisers. Google has two measures outside of click bid and your budget that play just as much of a role in how much traffic you get to your website: quality score and ad rank. If your website and ads suffer from noncompliance, Google may be artificially restricting how much traffic you are eligible to receive. This restriction may give your competitors an opportunity to overtake you in the marketplace and dominate traffic, even on your own product keywords.

Once you make all your advertising Google compliant, your quality scores and ad rank may have a major lift, and you may experience more traffic to your website than you have ever been able to buy to date. In some cases, the traffic may be so explosive and robust, if you haven't put up safeguards (such as restricting your daily budget from overspending or reducing your bids so the amount you are charged by Google is less), the increased advertising expenses may threaten your business as a whole, like what happened with James. Be prepared for total business transformation, not just in how you sell to customers on the website, but also how you manage your Google Ads account.

Once you have grown, stabilized, and transformed your business from this new, increased traffic, you will be ready to use the underground Google Ads traffic source only elite marketers are using to multiply their business exponentially. It is only reserved for the most trustworthy of Google Ads advertisers. Get ready, and enjoy the next chapter. It has the potential to change everything in your business.

CHAPTER THIRTEEN

Chapter 13

The Underground Google Ads Traffic Source Reserved

Only For the Most Trustworthy Advertisers

Five million dollars. That is the most money to date I have ever seen one of my clients spend within a single hour. When I looked at his "cost" column, I could not believe my eyes. One hour after launching his campaigns on Google's underground traffic network where only the most compliant advertisers are allowed to advertise, he had set the record for the most impressions, the most clicks, and the most conversions of clients I had ever had. He had more traffic and advertising spend in one hour than my largest client had ever done in a month. It was insanity. After I realized this was real and not a dream, I remember thinking, "I hope his check doesn't bounce."

You are probably wondering how in the world anyone can spend five million dollars in one hour on Google. Well, he was able to do this because he was granted access to Google's underground traffic network. Two weeks prior to this, we had a meeting and he told me his business was stuck. He had maxed out traffic on Google Ads, Facebook, Twitter, and Native, and didn't know where to go next to reach the next level in his business. He had an excellent website and product in the weight loss space, and had his sales process dialed in. All he was missing was more targeted traffic. He said he was thinking about going to mainstream media (TV ads, radio, and newspaper), but the return on investment (ROI) on that was horrible. He didn't really want to put the effort into these advertising channels for a small bump in sales.

This is when I suggested it was time to step up to the big leagues. He had been advertising compliantly for several years now, and had a firm grasp of what he could and could not do with his ads or website as it pertains to Google policy, so I felt comfortable suggesting he apply for access to the largest collection of premium website traffic on the planet right now: Google's programmatic buying platform, at the time called Google's DoubleClick Ad Network (now called Display and Video 360).

Google's programmatic buying platform is the traffic network behind the veil of Google Ads. It is unrestricted Google traffic, free from quality scores, ad ranks, and other means of determining how much traffic an advertiser can buy on Google. It is a pure auction and budget ecosystem, where you get traffic from all the premium websites you love, where the only thing that matters is what you are willing to pay for the traffic and how much of it you want. It is pure bliss. It is perfect capitalism! No outside forces, like quality score and ad rank to artificially affect the market—simply bid higher than your competitor and give the system a budget, and you will get all the traffic you want, seemingly endlessly.

Very few internet marketers know about programmatic buying, and even if they heard of it, even fewer know that Google owns their own programmatic buying network.

So what is programmatic buying? Andy Cocker, Co-founder of Infectious Media, defines programmatic buying as: "Programmatic Buying describes online display advertising that is aggregated, booked, flighted, analyzed and optimized via demand side software interfaces and algorithms. While it includes RTB it also includes non RTB methods and buy types such as Facebook Ads API and the Google Display Network. Programmatic also implies the use of multi sourced data signals to inform targeting and optimization decisions" (Define It - What is Programmatic Buying?, www.adexchanger.com, 2012).

In layman's terms, programmatic buying is like stock trading, but for advertising. Publishers have reserved spaces on their websites for ads (supply side of programmatic buying). When a visitor visits a landing page that has ad space reserved to serve ads, the publisher then acts like a floor trader at the stock exchange and starts crying out to ad networks (demand side of programmatic buying), "Hey, I got ad space to sell, I have a visitor right now and I will sell my ad space to the highest bidder!" In an instant, the ad networks began to bid and auction against one another for that ad space, trying to win the right to show an ad from one of their advertisers they have on their network.

This all happens on what is called an ad exchange (think of it like the New York Stock Exchange, but for ads). It reminds me of the crazy scenes on trading floors where people are screaming at one another and knocking over people, waving their hand in the air yelling, "I'll buy!" "Sell, sell, sell!" The only difference, really, between the stock exchange floor and programmatic buying is that this mosh pit of auction selling is all done electronically—and, of course, they are selling ads, not stocks. Demand-side programmatic platforms, such as Google's Display and Video 360, make their money by bidding for large blocks of ad spots on the ad exchange for their advertisers who need quality traffic.

The goal of this chapter isn't to give you a graduate-level understanding of programmatic buying and Google Display and Video 360. The purpose of this chapter is to let you know there is a higher level of Google traffic that you can't access by going through Google Ads. This source of traffic is the best and most pure internet traffic source available to marketers.

However, there is a catch...

It's only available to the most compliant internet advertisers, and your advertising budget needs to be very high on a monthly basis. On top of that, you usually have to sign a six- to twelve-month contract, guaranteeing your spend. To get access to Google's Display and Video 360 traffic, you need to have a history of clean advertising with no outstanding violations, and you can't promote a banned product. You also have to apply for access to the ad exchange through a trading desk (software agency that has access to ad exchanges). The trading desk may have monthly management fees as well, and they may take a percentage of what you spend. In addition, the ad exchanges charge the trading desk a data access fee that gets passed on to the advertisers. More importantly, the trading desk will screen your business model thoroughly to determine how risky you are to allow access to the ad exchanges through them.

If you can pass the compliance review, have a solid sales process, and have a large monthly budget, you may be able to get approved to access this traffic.

The client who spent five million dollars in one hour went on to earn fifty million dollars in revenue that year, shattering their previous yearly revenue total by more than forty million dollars. Being able to advertise on Google's Display and Video 360 Ad Exchange is the pinnacle of internet marketing. Elite marketers who have completed the journey of creating a Google-compliant website, Google-compliant ads, a transparent business model, and a large business will be eligible to apply to advertise on it. However, once you are approved, strap in, apply for an unlimited line of credit from your credit card company, and get ready for a traffic explosion experience unlike any other.

Summary

Once you are fully compliant, have a trustworthy advertising track record, and have maximized your sales on Google Ads, you are ready for Google's programmatic platform, Display and Video 360. This is the true Google traffic businesses dream of. Display and Video 360 is a true capitalist Ad Exchange. It is a pure auction system where you can get seemingly endless premium traffic from your favorite websites. Imagine being able to spend up to five million dollars a day on only the websites that convert best for your business like my client? What would your business look like today if you were able to access this underground traffic. By taking Google compliance seriously and implementing each part of this book, you will set yourself up to be able to take advantage of this platform when you are ready. Trustworthiness is the key. Once you are growing again on Google Ads with a compliant website, start creating a budgeting plan to handle a 10x growth daily growth in traffic. After you have sufficient reserves to handle this level of traffic and maxed out your growth on Google Ads, it is time to call 1-866-2-GOOGLE and request access to Display and Video 360. They will get you a list of their authorized agencies to begin your new journey.

CHAPTER FOURTEEN

Chapter 14

Final Thoughts

Although I poured my heart, soul, and all my knowledge into this book, this book will never be a complete summary of everything you will need to know to stay Google-compliant. Their policies change all the time, because the world is constantly changing. What may be inbounds and acceptable now may not be inbounds in the future—but by implementing everything you have learned in this book, you will help prevent Google from taking large scale, serious action against you.

Knowing the fundamentals of creating a compliant website will put you in a good place, so even if Google changes a policy that directly impacts you, they will give you a warning and time to change. If you don't get the changes right at first, they will simply ask you to make more corrective action with a disapproved ad. This is a far cry from getting your website banned—or even worse, your account banned.

The normal response from clients after learning this information is that it makes a lot of sense. Also, they claim they "kind of knew" this is what they needed to do, but there was so much misinformation about Google compliance, they weren't sure what steps actually worked. By using the tips in this book and drastically reducing your risk score, you will gain room to play around, split-test ideas, and add more controversial headlines in strategically placed locations, whereas before any little mistake could have triggered an account ban. This is the advantage to the system I have created for Google Ads compliance. By using the Hub Content site structure combined with attaching landing pages and their funnels, you can create a triple-win scenario for you, your buyer, and Google.

You're One Compliant Website Away

Since 2010, Google has invoiced my compliant clients four hundred million dollars. There is no way this can be done on any other internet marketing platform. When you think about scaling your business online, there really isn't any other source more capable than Google.

Your business will only be as successful as the amount of marketing you are able to drive into the marketplace, and one Google-compliant website is all that may be standing in the way between having an average business that struggles breaking through the glass ceiling and becoming the next business-success supernova. One compliant website will allow you to access traffic your competitors can only dream of getting because they don't know how to keep their ads up on Google, leaving you the solo big fish in a big pond.

Today, there are much fewer internet marketers on Google compared to when I first started back in 2009, because so many marketers are scared of getting banned. That loss of marketers has left a serious void of unmet needs for the consumer. One of the reasons so many people turned to Amazon to purchase goods is because of the lack of Google advertisers to meet the needs of the searcher. This has left vast, empty fields of uncultivated customers in need of a trustworthy Google marketer.

If you had just one compliant website, you could own all this fertile ground, unencumbered by competitors. The next growth wave is already here, and it's on Google Ads. There are more buyers on Google's ad networks than any other single source. In fact, there are more buyers than many of the top ad networks combined. A compliant website will get you access to Google Search, Google Display, YouTube, Gmail Ads, and the granddaddy Google traffic source of them all: Google Display & Video 360 (previously DoubleClick).

My last challenge to you, after you get back on Google, is to get the word out that it is possible to run on Google Ads again. Get my book in the hands of everyone who is an internet marketer. Make it required reading for your employees. Use it as a free gift at the conferences you put on. If I am going to change the world of marketers for the better, I can think of no better way than to have ten thousand internet marketers find their way back to Google Ads compliantly.

Thank you for reading. I look forward to seeing your success—and I look forward to seeing your ads!

Acknowledgments

First and foremost, I would like to thank God for giving me the strength and grace to write this book. With God, all things are possible.

With the same level of humility, love, and joy, I want to thank my family for allowing me to put our lives on a temporary hold while I wrote this book during one of the worst pandemics in US history. Thank you for allowing me to fulfill my dream of reaching the world with a book of hope and change, for the purposes of helping internet marketers around the world obtain the success they deserve.

To my wife, Joni, who has stood by me during every success, every failure, every sleepless night, and every moment of joy—thank you for giving me the courage to expand my impact on the world. And to my two sons, Isiah and Dion, and my two daughters, Kiah and Vivia, thank you for being my inspiration and hope during this process and giving me the boldness to continue to grow, so I may continue to earn that wonderful name that every man aspires to hear from their children: "Father."

Lastly, to the hundreds of business owners I have worked with through the years, thank you for allowing me into your businesses to consult and assist you with Google Ads compliance. I know how much of a leap of faith it was to trust a stranger with the future of your companies. Because of that trust, I can take the lessons I learned in helping your businesses comply with Google's policies to teach the world how to do the same.

Author Bio

Dathen Fairley is considered by many business experts to be the world's foremost independent expert on Google Ads policy. After having his first successful affiliate marketing business suspended by Google, he fought to get his account reinstated and accomplished this in less than one month. Since then, he has been on a crusade to prevent other marketers from getting their Google Ads accounts suspended. Since opening his first compliance consulting business in October 2009, he has helped hundreds of small, medium, and large business owners navigate through the rules and regulations of Google policy. In 2010, he started his first of three digital marketing agencies, and has since managed over four hundred million dollars in Google Ads spending. He is based out of Dayton, Ohio.

To learn more about his recent projects or how to contact his companies, go to www.DathenFairley.com.

Thank You for Reading My Book!

I'd love to hear your honest opinion.

Customer Questions & Answers

Q Have a question? Search for answers

Typical questions asked about products:
- Is the item durable?
- Is this item easy to use?
- What are the dimensions of this item?

Customer Reviews

There are no customer reviews yet.

5 star
4 star
3 star
2 star
1 star

Share your thoughts with other customers

Write a customer review

Please leave a review on Amazon so others can read what you thought of the book and make an informed purchasing decision about the usefulness of the information in this book.

Thank you so much!

Dathen Fairley

Made in United States
Troutdale, OR
10/25/2023

14012942R00137